Cody is a writer from the woods of Maine. After being discharged from the Marine Corps in 2016 with a Post-Traumatic Brain Injury, he came home to sort his shattered life out and accidentally became a writer. He holds his MFA from Stonecoast in creative writing and spends his time wandering in forest and collecting stories.

For my grandma, Sara, and all the mentors I had along the way.

Cody Mower

STRANGER IN MY OWN SKIN

AUSTIN MACAULEY PUBLISHERS™

LONDON • CAMBRIDGE • NEW YORK • SHARJAH

Ordering Information
Quantity sales: Special discounts are available on quantity purchases by corporations, associations, and others. For details, contact the publisher at the address below.

Publisher's Cataloging-in-Publication data
Mower, Cody
Stranger in My Own Skin

ISBN 9781685623807 (Paperback)
ISBN 9781685623814 (ePub e-book)

Library of Congress Control Number: 2023911208

www.austinmacauley.com/us

First Published 2023
Austin Macauley Publishers LLC
40 Wall Street, 33rd Floor, Suite 3302
New York, NY 10005
USA

mail-usa@austinmacauley.com
+1 (646) 5125767

I'd like to thank Austin Macauley for giving me an opportunity to share this story with the world.

Chapter One:
2016

It is six o'clock in the morning. Before conscious thoughts have a chance to twist me up, I am already filled with foreboding. The North Carolina sun is still hidden behind the horizon. I get dressed, grabbing the folded uniform I keep next to the couch. In typical Marine Corps fashion, by the time I'm dressed, it's only four minutes past six. I still don't have anywhere to be for another hour and a half. Base traffic can get hairy by seven, but I decide not to wake Sara up until six-thirty, giving her and Cameron time to sleep in. I hate this part of the day. It is a scripted dance between us, where I had to ask permission to go to work, and she reluctantly agrees. I know every word that is about to be said. Rolling over into the couch, pressing my face against the cushions, I struggle to breathe in the hot fabric. Picturing myself fading into the dark, never having to wake up to this misery again. But I always pull away.

My phone buzzes on the floor. I don't like to use my cane inside the house, so I used one hand on the wall to keep balance as I walked down the hallway. It's a short space between Cameron's room to Sara's door. Every morning that I push it open, it feels like I was pushing into a wound. Keeping it fresh. Somedays, I want to break it off its hinges.

Most days, I wanted to brick it up, so she can stay on the other side forever. But today, I push it open because I don't want to get written up for being late.

"Sara?" I ask into the darkness.

No reply.

"Sara?" I say again, leaning through the doorway.

"What!?" The sharpness in her tone made me queasy.

"I have work."

"Okay, can you please leave so I can get dressed?" This time she sounded more like herself. Refrained. Distant.

"Yeah," I said, "I'll get Cameron up."

"No."

"No, what?" I asked.

"Don't get him up. I'll do it."

"Why? I can't wake up my own son. Am I too incompetent to help around the house?" I hiss into shadows.

Nothing.

"I'll get him up. Go start the car or something, and we'll be out in a minute."

"Whatever."

I make my way back down to the couch to put my boots on. Bending over to lace up the worn suede, I catch a glimpse of Sara coming out to get Cameron dressed. Her hair had become a constant mess of brown threads, and her skin was growing pale from never leaving the house. She always wore black. Everywhere. Every day. As if being married to me was a death sentence. Mourning. Some nights, I could hear her talking to her stepdad about me on the phone. I could never hear all the words. I knew she was making fun of me. Talking about my cane, talking about my stupid mistakes, I knew she was laughing at me because of how far I had fallen. Some nights, when the house was quiet, I could hear her crying. I was already sitting in the car when Sara came out of the house with our half-asleep son in her arms. In the golden glow of the new morning, I could see him looking at me, smiling. I smiled back and wondered if he knew anything that has happened between Sara and me? Had he learned something devastating, listening through the walls? Could he comprehend the pain in this house?

Pulling out of the driveway, Sara and I settled into our routine. She kept her eyes on the road, and I kept my face turned towards the window. Very rarely did we say anything to one another. The dead air left to be filled by the radio or Cameron's babbling. Today though, something had been on my mind, and I wanted to at least put it out in the open.

"The medical board will be back with my results soon. The doc says the traumatic brain injury and a handful of other stuff are on there. He is pretty sure I should be getting out this summer," I said, still looking out the window.

"Okay."

"What are we going to do?" I asked, already regretting the question

I could tell the word *we* sounded as awful to her as it did to me. There was no more *we*, and there hadn't been for a long time.

"I don't know, Cody. I'm not really thinking about it," she said, merging into the long line of trucks and cars crawling their way through the front gate of Camp Lejeune.

"Okay, well, figure it out because I have to put down where I want all my shit sent to, and it would be nice to know where that is," I said.

"It's more complicated than that."

"Is it?" I asked. "You either want to work it out, or you don't."

"That's just it," she said, looking over at me, "Somedays, I can't stand to look at you. All I think about is Amie and the lies. Other days I really want to make this work because I think I still love you."

"You either love me, or you don't, Sara," I said, shifting the cane between my legs. "We have been over everything, we've fought, argued, and I *thought* we moved past some things."

"Me too."

"You knew what that was. I'm so sick of you treating it like I was some sort of bad guy. I was scared, Sara. I knew something was wrong with me, and I asked you to hold my hand through it. I fucking cried on the stairs in Midway, BEGGING you to help me because I needed you."

Silence.

"Remember?" I said.

Sara continued to drive through traffic as if nothing was happening, and I couldn't contain myself. Swinging around in my seat, I felt the heat rise in my face as I started to talk louder.

"You looked me dead in the face and told me to get a psychologist because you couldn't help me. So, EXCUSE ME, for talking to someone who actually pretended to listen."

In the back seat, Cameron covered his ears, making faces in the dark.

"Can you please stop yelling?"

I shook my head in disbelief as we pulled up to the gate. Nothing was ever her fault. Cody would always and forever be the asshole that went outside the marriage. The broken mess of a man who destroyed our family. If that is how she wanted me to be, then fuck it, why not? Why not be the monster she kept treating me as.

"Whatever," I said, settling back in my seat. "Can you pull into Dunkin before dropping me off? I don't want to make Sweeney drive me again."

"Yeah, sure," she said. "Not a problem."

It took thirty minutes to get through the traffic and to the front of the Battalion Headquarters to drop me off. Back when Sara and I were still openly trying to work things out, this was the point where I would turn to her and say something like, "I love you." Something encouraging, something that sounded like hope, but those days ended months ago.

"I'll see you at five," I said, getting out of the car.

"Stop giving me time," she said, rolling her eyes. "I'm tired of you telling me to be here at five or four-thirty, and I get here just to wait in the parking lot for another forty-five minutes."

"Fine," I said, "I'll call you when I'm off work."

"Okay."

"Thanks for stopping so I could get coffee."

She nodded.

"Bye."

"Bye."

Leaning on my cane, I watched her pull out of the parking lot. It is strange to think that there was a time where we would have held on a little longer. An uncomfortable memory. Every time she left, I felt a sense of relief, and I think so did she. Opening the doors to headquarters, I made my way to the company office. Our building didn't have an elevator for the handicap, so with one hand on my cane and the other filled with cold brew, I leaned forward. Teeter-tottering up each step, keeping my left shoulder on the wall, like a drunk. I had to take a minute to collect my strength at the top before walking into the company office where Gunny White was sitting behind his desk, looking at his watch.

"Sergeant Mower, good of you to join us this morning," he said in a soft voice.

I took a seat on the small couch in his office. I already knew what was coming.

"You're late," he said, tapping his desk with a ball-point pen, "That's twice this week."

"Sorry, Gunny, I'm having problems at home," I said.

He pointed at my coffee. "You got to Dunkin just fine.

"Last chance, Mower," he said, leaning back in his chair. "Get out. Go back to the barracks and wait for word. If you're late again, I'm going to page eleven your ass, understand? And for someone trying to get out, the last thing you want is negative paperwork."

"Yes, Gunny," I said, standing back up. Halfway to the door, he stopped me.

"If you're having trouble, we have a crisis hotline to call. Don't bring it into work."

Good talk, I thought.

Chapter Two:
The Thing in the Mirror

May 24th, 2017, 11am

Waking up, I could tell that the hangover was going to be bad. My eyes hadn't even opened yet, and the mattress was already swimming underneath me. The pitch and roll of the bed mixed with the stench of stale whiskey clinging to the back of my teeth. With half-opened eyes, my gaze tumbled from the wall. Holy Shit. This isn't my apartment. My heart beat in a heavy, sluggish rhythm, adrenaline failing to fire; I was stuck in half-panic. The room was sparsely furnished, save a wrinkled brown tapestry pinned to the wall, and I was alone in a four-poster bed with nothing but a blanket that reeked of sweat. Patting myself down, I noticed I was still fully dressed, only missing my shoes. I couldn't feel my wallet, keys, and cellphone. My pockets were completely empty. If I had been robbed, there was nothing that could be done about it now.

Six years of Marine Corps' training awakened within me, and I began looking for weapons and an escape route. There wasn't much for weapons. I thought I could roll up a calendar I saw hanging on the wall to get in some jabs at someone's throat, but quickly discarded the idea. There were only two exits that I could see. A closed door to my left and the windows in front of me. The swaying floor beneath my feet reminded me I was in no condition to fight; escape was the best option. Creeping as quietly as I could towards the window, the world tipped a bit too far to the left, and I lost balance, crashing onto the hardwood.

My body ached in a twisted heap on the floor as the room began to sway like an old bridge. Panicked thoughts started screaming their way through my head. Pulling myself over to the window ledge, I peeked out from behind the curtain. I was on the first floor of a building with an empty driveway. Okay, I can do this, I thought. The bright light poured on to my face and made me dry heave. Pushing the window up, humid air brushed past me and into the room. The wooden frame cracked under my weight as I began to make my escape. I was half-way out of the window when the door slowly creaked open behind me. A familiar voice filled the room.

"Cody?" it said in hushed worry.

"Courtney?" I asked. With some effort, I rolled myself back into the room, taking small strips of white paint from the windowsill with me. Sinking onto the floor, I felt the dry heave return.

"Yeah," she said, pushing open the door. I would have recognized that tangled mess of red hair anywhere: Courtney Ellis, one of the few friends I had made since moving to Portland. *What is she doing here?*

She crossed the room to shut the window, turned, and took a seat next to me on the floor. "Are you okay?"

"Um, yeah, I guess?" I lied. "What happened?"

"Ryan and I brought you back to our house last night. You were pretty trashed, but don't worry, your stuff is next to the bed." She pointed to my phone and wallet.

"What?" The last thing I remembered was playing pool in the billiard hall and laughing with some tourists from the UK, trying not to talk about Sara. There were flashes of the night sky and sidewalks, but nothing else I could make out.

"Yeah, Ryan and I met you at Old Port Tavern last night, remember?" she said, putting a small hand on my shoulder. Her breath smelled like vodka and cigarettes. "We didn't think it was safe for you to be left alone in your…state."

"Oh," I said. I wanted to say something else, but the slosh of beer and whiskey turned over in my stomach. "Where's your bathroom?"

Bent over the toilet bowl, I stuck my hands into my mouth and tried to empty what alcohol I had left in my stomach. When I had finished, I spat what chunks I had left floating in my mouth and brushed my teeth with a spare toothbrush. I met Courtney in her kitchen. I took a seat at the table, which was overflowing with empty beer bottles and an assortment of crystal ashtrays that reeked of old weed. There was hardly room to put my head in my hands. Bare windows filtered the morning sunlight through vodka bottles that crowded the sagging windowsill, throwing out a kaleidoscope of fractals that stung my eyes.

"I'm so fucking sorry," I groaned as Courtney placed a fresh cup of coffee in front of me. I watched the steam rise and disappear into the air. She leaned back on the cluttered countertop with a mug of water and smiled.

"Oh, sweetie," she laughed, waving me off, "we've all been there, you were so fun, you kept saying that…"

"No, please!" I said, holding up a shaking hand in embarrassment, "Please, no stories…my ego can't take it."

I couldn't count how many times I had threatened to kick the shit out of obnoxious bar-goers or how many women had to listen to me pour my stupid heart out about my military service. I would rather just be left in the dark.

"Well, that's fine," she said, pulling out the only other chair at the table.

"At least, tell me…I wasn't awful, was I?" I asked, knowing I didn't want to hear the answer.

"God, no, you were a perfect gentleman the whole night. It was kind of cute," she said, running her hands through my hair.

It was the only sense of relief I had that morning. I took a sip from my coffee cup. There was a time when I hadn't need alcohol to be social. After Sara left me, though, that changed. When I wasn't drinking, I felt empty and irritated by the world around me. I could hardly think of a reason to get out of bed sober. Even if I was starving, I would just try to sleep or watch YouTube until the bars opened. Only when I had whiskey in my blood did I actually feel something close to normal again.

"Where's Ryan?" I asked. I'd only noticed that I hadn't seen her boyfriend yet, which was odd considering they were almost joined at the hip out in public.

"He left for work hours ago," she said with a shrug.

"Shit, what time is it?" I pulled out my phone, but the black screen didn't change; it must have died in the night.

"Past eleven," Courtney said, checking hers. "You want me to call an Uber or something?"

"That depends," I said, slumping over. "I have no idea where your house is."

I had begun to sober up and became painfully aware of a pounding headache developing, thanks to dehydration. So, that's why she has water, I thought. I wanted to ask for some but couldn't impose any more than I already had.

Pulling up a map on her phone, Courtney plotted points from her place in the West End to my apartment on Congress Street. I squinted at the screen, trying to make sense of the data. It looked as though I was only half a mile from my apartment, which was a ten-minute walk at most. On any other day, this would have been a nice brisk walk through town, but today, that half-mile looked like a marathon.

Nauseated at the idea of doing anything else but hiding in a dark hole, I lied and told her walking would be fine.

"Be careful, yeah?" she said with a wink.

Walking back to the apartment, trying to avoid the blinding light of the sun, I kept my head down, face to face with the worn red brick sidewalks Portland was known for. As nauseous as I was feeling in the baking heat, it didn't compare to Camp Lejeune. Looking down at my shoes, I found it strange that only a year ago, they were tan combat boots begrudgingly making their way to formation instead of a shower. My stomach churned in large nauseating circles, forcing me to take a break in the thin shade of a weather-beaten telephone pole. My vision began to blur along the edges, but it was too late to ask for help. The sidewalk, twisted from centuries of harsh Maine winters, carried my stumbling corpse under the sighing arches and painted doorways of the many 20th-century Gothic revival style buildings, like shit down a picturesque river. Taking the only turn in my route, I was relieved to be on Congress Street. At least this walk of shame wouldn't seem out of place on Portland's main drag, which was filled with a mix of alcoholic college kids and drug addicts.

I passed the 7/11 when the ground shifted violently under my feet, sending me in awkwardly looping side steps. My shoulder crashed into a cast iron streetlamp, which kept me from spilling onto the road. Every tender point in my body was ringing with pain as I collected myself. Standing back up, I felt the gaze of a middle-aged white woman burning through me as she gassed up her white Land Rover. When my eyes met hers, I knew exactly the kind of look she was giving me. Disgust. Something I'd seen too many times before. Glaring back at her, I stumbled on. Fuck her. She didn't know the first thing about me.

When I medically retired from the Marine Corps, a large part of it had been because of a traumatic brain injury (TBI), which I had sustained during what was supposed to be an easy deployment. When our battalion touched down in Okinawa, the island was wrapped in the colors of night, dotted with the ugly amber lights of the base, hiding the deep emerald jungle and transparent sapphire infused waters that lapped away at unmolested sand beaches. A vacation deployment, they called it. For the first few months, it really did seem that way. Training on the weekdays, hitching rides on Blackhawks, which moved slowly against the azure skies. Our company got ordered up to the continent for an exchange program with the marines of South Korea. I was rappelling down a cliff – it was an exercise. I was harnessed, safe from danger. A misstep. A brief moment of negligence on the rappel had me seeing stars. I was okay. It was just a bump on the head, right?

I took up scuba to get my certification with PADI Divers in my free time, but I couldn't catch a break-even in trying to relax. On my final dive, a chance encounter with a cave wall shut my air off. I panicked. Blacked out. Woke up on the surface with a terrified dive partner. Within a few weeks, I had developed crippling vertigo along with a whole host of other problems. None of which I found any sympathy for in my unit. All the heroic and validating reasons for injury, getting blown up by an IED, getting shot at by the enemy, hell even rolling over in a Humvee, were not a part of my story. Because of that, I had to suffer that same look of disgust from higher-ups who reserved injuries only for the noble, for real heroes. It was a compounding shame that ate away at me.

Heroes don't get hurt on vacation.

Shambling forward once more over the uneven brick, I cursed the streetlamp for saving my ass from the onslaught of cars in the road. Every part of me hurt. Years of abuse in the infantry wreaked havoc on my joints. The insides of my hip felt like they were shredding themselves apart. Reaching the door of my apartment building, I found myself once again needing to take a break. Sitting in the shade of the giant steel awning, I pressed my back up against the cold stone of the wall and shivered. My head was still swimming as I stared at the massive brick building across the street, with its many rows of identical square windows. My vision lazily falling from window to window, it finally hit the ground where I saw two doors that I had never noticed before.

Less than a foot apart from each other and only separated by a sliver of a green wooden beam, they were both made of identical glass. Above the left door was a large metal sign, which read Optimal Self, and from what I could see through the glass, a gym. The door on the right had no sign but said in large printed letters: The Jewel Box Blues Bar, which made me laugh. Was that some sort of high-road, low-road joke? Revived slightly by my laughter, I peeled myself off the ground and headed into my building.

A sudden blast of air conditioning took the edge off my misery as I opened up the door. Standing in the lobby, I wondered whether or not it was acceptable to just sleep on the floor like the homeless do whenever they manage to sneak in. Eyeing the stiff fake leather couches, I decided against it and took the cement stairs up to the studio apartment I shared with my younger brother. Casey and I had shared a room growing up, and when we moved into the city for school, we decided that a studio would do us just fine.

It was cozy, with three grey walls, the fourth painted a bizarre shade of muted teal. Off to the left was a small but modern kitchen with wooden cupboards and cramped counter space. The kitchen also had a spacious walk-in closet next to the fridge, which we used for storage. At the end of the kitchen was the bathroom that crammed a standing shower, sink, and toilet in only seven square feet of grey tiles. The only furniture we owned was a handmade bookshelf, two cheap L-shaped desks, Frankensteined into one 'mega desk', and a set of swivel chairs that had been on sale at the local Staples. With the desks and the bookshelf taking up so much of the floor space, there wasn't room for a bed, let alone two. I slept on a beanbag in the window ledge, and Casey had an air mattress that folded up into a nook in the wall. Simple. If not elegant.

Breathing heavily from the walk up the stairs, I had to double-check to make sure this was our place as I struggled to put the keys in the lock. Pushing the door open, I was greeted by darkness and the soft glow of a computer screen. Flipping the lights on revealed that the place was empty. A yellow sticky note was tacked to Casey's laptop screen, which read: *Gone to Hannah's Be Back Later. Sorry About The Hangover.*

"Alright then," I said to myself, crumpling up the note and throwing it onto the floor. I didn't want him to see me like this anyway. In the few months we lived together, he'd had to walk my drunk ass home at one in the morning or deal with my post-binge vomiting in the kitchen more than he should have. At least I could spare him this time. After shuffling out of my sweaty, whiskey-stained clothes, I chugged a few large glasses of water before cranking the knob in the shower all the way up.

Waiting for the water to get hot, I lay half-naked on the kitchen floor, trying to erase from my thoughts the face of that sneering woman at 7/11, with no success.

Defeated, I crawled my way into the bathroom and locked the door behind me. The mix of heat and moisture filling the room didn't feel great, but I convinced myself, like every other time, that it was purging the alcohol from my pores. Climbing into the hot water, I couldn't keep myself from swaying side to side and so squatted into the fetal position. The shower was so small that I had just enough room to flex one ankle at a time. At least if I fall asleep, it will be impossible for me to drown, I thought. My skin cried out as the scalding water beat down on my hunched over body, but I didn't move. Ribbons of water snaked their way around my toes and emptied down into the drain.

I don't remember passing out, but I must have at some point because I was startled awake by a falling shampoo bottle that caused me to jerk and hit my head against the hard-plastic wall. The steam had cleared my sinuses, and for the first time, I could taste how revolting my breath was. It was almost enough to make me sick all over again.

I need to brush my teeth and go back to bed, I thought.

I tried to stand back up, but my legs were asleep. *Goddamn it*. Shutting the water off, I pushed open the shower door, letting a rush of air shock my wet skin. It took a minute for the pins and needles to subside before I could finally get up and grab a towel. My hands were so wrinkled, they felt alien to me as I wiped away the fog from the mirror. In the clouded glass, two button-eyes lifelessly watched me from inside purple-rimmed sockets. My dehydrated mind went blank, not recognizing the face in the reflection.

I cleared away another round of fog from the glass and took one more step back to get a better look at the naked body in the mirror. It was a window onto horrors. On the other side, a humanoid creature followed my every movement, its waxy skin stretching like yellowed parchment over its torso. Its entire rib cage was on display. I followed it all the way up with wide eyes until the sweeping collar bone framed the ghastly image from behind its skin. Reaching towards the glass, it mimicked me, touching its face with my bloated fingers. Exhaling, I turned my back to the mirror, and the creature copied me once again. My heart pounded, and my hands started trembling as I closed them into a fragile fist. I could no longer bear to look at the thing in the mirror. I wrapped myself up in a towel and shut the light off, and sat in the dark on the cold floor.

Facing the wall, I could feel the air escaping out of my lungs. What was that? My chest spasmed as I tried to gasp for air. Oh my God, that's me. Tears stung my eyes, and I choked on the shame that erupted in my throat. No, please. I spun around and went back to the mirror, wiping the fog away in the dark. I could feel the same hollowed eyes glaring at me from the other side. I collapsed onto the toilet seat and held my head in my hands; the truth of the moment overwhelmed me. The drinking, the late nights, and the hate had worn through my soul and into my body. I was no longer able to hide from myself. My mind convulsed as I thought of Sara and Cameron, of the cold, of all the therapy sessions; it hit me that I was not 'okay,' as I was pretending to be. Even after moving to the city, going to school, starting life anew, I was still rotting, both inside and out.

My legs felt unsteady as I walked back to my desk chair. Turning my hands over, I thought of all the things they had done in the last three years. How many bottles had they held? How many times did they miss a chance to hold my son? To comfort my wife? How many times have they pushed away all that had meant something to me? Shaking, I looked up at the glass case on my bookshelf, which held the folded flag I was handed during my retirement ceremony.

"I DON'T WANNA BE THIS ANYMORE, I DON'T WANT TO!" I screamed into the empty room, crying in incoherent pain. For five minutes, I stood at its edge. Then I slumped down, exhausted, into the chair.

"I don't want to be ashamed anymore," I whispered at last. Collecting myself, I got dressed in silence. Pulling a shirt over my head, I thought about the gym I had seen earlier across the street, Optimal Self. Making the decision on a whim, I thought that if I couldn't change my body's inside, maybe I could do something about the outside. Not wanting to return to the bathroom, I rinsed my mouth out with some cold coffee Casey had left on the counter to cover the smell of whiskey on my breath and headed out.

Pushing the glass door open, I was struck by the smell of rubber and sweat. The walls were painted a vibrant blue, but what caught my attention was a set of four white square pillars that supported a large balcony attached to the second floor. Each side of the pillars bore a single word painted in silver letters: Justice, Judgement, Dependability…fourteen words in all, and I knew them intimately. These were the fourteen leadership traits I had learned in the service. A handful of people moved around the cramped space, shifting weights, seemingly unaware of my presence. Above the squat racks on my right, a large American flag and black POW flag were the only decorations on the wall, and I knew immediately that whoever owned this gym was a veteran. My heart jumped at the idea of meeting another vet, but that excitement was quickly smothered by doubt. What if they find out about my injury? What's going to happen when I tell them I didn't get hurt doing anything special? Are they going to give me that same look of contempt? Of disgust?

As I fought myself alone on the threshold, my feet didn't move. They stood rooted to a small patch of tile, making the decision for me.

Chapter Three:
Optimal Self

May 24th 2017, 1:18pm

I was hit with the smell of sweat and rubber mats. A dark-haired man and petite woman talked in the corner; their conversation lost in the deep rhythm of tribal music that flowed from the speakers. But as the door shut and the bell dinged behind me, it managed to draw the attention of both of them. The man pardoned himself and made his way past the series of iron squat racks. He had an intimidating frame but extended his heavily tattooed arm with such gentleness it caught me off guard.

"I'm Eric, this is my gym," he said, smiling.

"Cody," I said, shaking his hand.

"Cody, what branch of service were you in?"

The question startled me. I guess there was no point in hiding. Let the judging begin. But I wondered what gave it away? My tattoos? Or how I carried my shattered stoicism around with the little pride I had left. I hadn't expected to be called out so soon.

"I was in the Marine Corps," I said, fighting my hangover. "Infantry. I'm a medically retired sergeant." The words just sort of came out. My chest tightened. *I didn't mean to say that.* I thought, *you fucking idiot.*

"A Marine? That's awesome. I was in the Army, 18 Delta, medic. Got out as a Staff Sergeant," he said.

"Special Forces, that's badass," I said, still waiting for the hammer to drop. The inevitable questioning about my injury. The inevitable rejection.

"You want to come upstairs, and we can talk about what you want to do here?" he asked.

"Uh, yeah, sure," I said. I felt an obligation to go with him, even though I was beginning to question having shown up in the first place. My hands had started to sweat, and I wiped them off on my shorts. This was moving too fast for me, but I had been the one to walk into his place.

We walked across the gym's rubber mats to the narrow set of wooden stairs that led to the open office, which looked down over the gym like the view from a throne. Eric motioned for me to take a seat on a futon he pressed against the wall while he grabbed a swivel chair from his desk. The office was cozy and filled with plants. From the windowsill to ivy-covered railings, the whole place felt a world apart from the sweat and the iron downstairs.

"Tell me what going on with you, bro?" he said, crossing his arms. "I'm not here to judge, but I've seen that hungover look before. Veteran to veteran, are you okay?"

I searched his face for an alternative motive, but everything told me this was a question he wanted a real answer for. I have always been a guarded person. Even after Sara left me, I didn't let the rest of my family know that it had bothered me. I always felt the more someone knew about you, the more ammunition they had to use against you, but something about Eric was different. I trusted him. It was entirely irrational, but I couldn't help it. Maybe it was the way he was leaning forward in his chair to listen. The alarming disarmament of my fear worried me. But my gut told me that he wouldn't care. Looking around the room, it took me a moment to focus on his question and just how big it was. With the hangover perched heavily on the front of my brow, I just let the truths spill out.

"I've spent three years getting healthy in the mind and heart," I said. "I got a brain injury and basically ruined my life with bad decisions. My wife left and took our son with her." I wanted to shut the words off, but they just kept coming out. "I took the pills, went to therapy, and accepted the past for what it was, and I thought it was enough." My voice was starting to crack. "But today, I noticed something." Tears began to sting my eyes as I looked down at my hands. "I still have this rot inside me, and I was looking out the window of my apartment, and I thought that maybe…" I couldn't finish my sentence. Though somehow, after that, I felt lighter.

Eric sat back in his chair, studying me for a moment. Over his shoulder, the citation for his bronze star on the wall caught the light flooding through the window, and I began to seep back into reality.

Putting his hand on my shoulder, he said "Don't worry, we can fix that."

"How?" I asked, trying to compose myself.

"Do you remember in your training, the mind, body, spirit, mentality?" he asked, reaching on his desk for a cup of coffee. I knew what he was talking about from my time in the Marine Corps as foundations for the Warrior Mindset.

Part of the knowledge they drill into your head from boot camp on, which said that the three aspects of a person, mind, body, and spirit, are all intimately connected and that balancing these three concepts promoted the proper fighting spirit.

"Yeah, I remember, but usually, it was used as an excuse to haze us on the softball field with training, strengthening the body, they said."

"That's because the military had a hard time knowing what is actually good for people," he said, taking a sip of his coffee.

"Tell me about it," I said, leaning back into the futon. Wiping my eyes with the back of my hand to make sure the tears were dry, I cleared my throat.

"Do you want some coffee, bro?" Eric asked, standing up.

"Actually, I would love some if that's alright," I said.

Eric leaned over the railing. "Hey Ben!" he yelled.

"Yeah?" came a heavy voice from down below.

"Can you bring me a cup of coffee, please?"

"Black?"

"Yes, please," he said. "Cody, you have to meet Ben. He's been coming here for a while now. Super cool guy. When you get the chance, you'll have to lift with him."

After a moment, one of the largest men I had ever met came up the stairs holding what looked to be a tiny cup of coffee.

"Ben, this is Cody. He'll be joining us soon," Eric said, motioning to me.

"Oh, cool!" Ben said, his gigantic arms outstretched for a handshake. "You'll like it here, alright, I don't mean to run, but I really have to get on my next set."

"Good to meet you, good luck," I said, taking my coffee. "Thank you."

Ben smiled and headed back downstairs.

It was odd to be having such a pleasant conversation with a stranger. Eric wheeled around in his chair and thought for a moment.

"Where was I?" he asked out into the air. "Sorry, I have a brain injury too, and I can lose track of things pretty easily." He pointed at the seven sticky notes tacked to his computer monitor. "I use this to remind myself of the day's chores."

It was reassuring to know that Eric and I shared something in common.

"Me too," I said. "You were saying something about hazing? I think?"

"OH!" he said, snapping his fingers, "Mind, body, and spirit is the approach we take at Optimal Self." Leaning back, he gestured over the railing to the weight room below, "Total health is not just about how strong you are. You need to focus on yourself as a whole being."

"Makes sense," I said, "I don't know how to do that."

"Everyone's path is different, but from the looks of you," Eric cleared his throat, "And I mean this with no judgment attached, okay? It's just my observation is that you have neglected your body for a long time."

I looked down at my shaking legs and thought about what I had seen in the mirror. Eric was right, of course. I had done all I could to get off the cane, but that was an ego choice, not because I wanted to get healthier. I just didn't want people to think I was a soft target and try to rob me.

"Yeah, I get that," I said. "You're not wrong."

"I think one of the best things you can do now is to pay some attention to the physical side of it and see what comes to you. We can work on the other stuff too while you're here if you want."

"I'm down for working on the physical part, but," I hesitated, "I don't know how much emotional and spiritual strength I'm working with if I'm honest." I took a deep breath. "All therapy did was get me to a point where I was 'okay' with living with myself, which is good, but I don't know, man. I don't want to be a downer."

Eric smiled. "Listen, bro, I've been there too, trust me, I have, but something pushed you here. Right through those doors and into the gym. You have to trust that some part of you, even if it's buried, knows that you're worth saving, or getting better, or however you want to put it."

My brain couldn't wrap itself around those words. The idea that some glowing part of me was still trying to rise to the surface baffled me.

"Alright, man, yeah, okay, let's do this," I said, laying back into the futon.

Eric reached around into his desk and pulled out a few pieces of paper.

"Before we discuss a way forward, I need to lay down one simple ground-rule," his voice grew stern, effortlessly switching his tone into one brimming with military command. "Are you listening?"

"Yes, sir," I said instinctively.

"If you ever come into this gym either hungover or drunk again, I'm going to ask you to leave."

I could feel the embarrassment rack my body.

"Some people here are working very hard to be sober, and coming in smelling like whiskey isn't doing them any favors, okay?"

"Yes, sir."

"It's nothing against you, but try to be considerate of the others in the room."

"I'm sorry, I just…" I thought for a minute. "No, you're right, no excuses," I said, shutting my mouth tightly.

"Hey, if you want to go to a meeting and talk about it then I can point you in the right direction. But from one vet to another, let me tell you whiskey isn't worth it." Eric reached over, grabbed his car keys, and tossed them into my lap so I could see the Alcoholics Anonymous chips proudly dangling from them. I got the hint.

Sitting in the chair staring into my coffee, I thought hard over Eric's words and the astronomic impossibility that I lived across from a gym where the owner was someone who knew where I was coming from. I wanted to get better, even if I didn't know what better looked like. I at least had to start somewhere.

"No, I don't need to go to a meeting, but thank you," I said. "Let me try doing it myself. To be honest with you, I haven't even tried to stop since leaving my grandmother's house, and I hate the hangovers."

"Your grandma lives in Portland?"

"No, uh, when Sara left me, she stayed in Pennsylvania, and I moved into my grandmother's attic, stayed there for nine months before I was ready to show my face in public."

I laughed. "Now I live across the street with my brother, and I'm going to school at the University of Southern Maine."

"Oh, that's good. What are you studying?"

"English," I said. "I love books, reading, and writing. All that boring stuff. I don't know what I'm going to do with it, but I found myself drawn to the field."

Eric smiled wide and shook his head.

"What?" I said.

"You mean to tell me, you crawled from a broken marriage to live in an attic, got yourself well enough to go to school, and you're now studying something you enjoy?" he said. "You've done all of that, and you mean to tell me you've given up on yourself?"

My brain halted. No one had ever said it like that before.

"Uh, maybe?" I tripped over my own thoughts.

"I'm telling you right now, bro, there is something in you that is pushing you forward. You weren't meant to live your life how you have been," he said. "You need to trust that you are meant for better things."

Part of me really did want to believe in what Eric was saying, but the hands of cynicism were still holding onto me.

"You sound like my grandma."

"Maybe your grandma is a wise woman."

When I had finished my coffee, I made the commitment to at least try to stop drinking cold turkey for the rest of June. I had never attempted it before. I heard it was rough, but Eric promised that if I ever needed to talk, he would help me through it and that I was welcome to come to sit in the gym in the massage chair to get my mind off of the craving should it arrive. I signed a contract committing to six months at Optimal Self. Eric waived the forty-dollar signup fee and gave me a plan to start working out beginning tomorrow after I had sobered up. On my way out the door, he gave me his cellphone number and told me that his phone was on, just in case. I thanked him and headed back out into the humidity.

The door to the apartment slammed behind me as I made my way to my chair. The hangover was beginning to subside. I sat in silence for a few minutes before I noticed that Casey was home. Taking off his headphones, he looked at me.

"How was the gym?" he asked. I stared at the wall a moment longer before answering.

"How'd you know I went to the gym? You spying on me?"

Casey laughed. "No, I saw you standing in the doorway from the window. I guess I had just missed you leaving."

"Oh. Shit. It was alright," I said. My thoughts were still churning over Eric's words. And trying to figure out how in a single conversation, I managed to grow this fragile whisper of hope that I had not had in years. I was gripped by fear that if I were to speak its name out loud, this precious gift would shatter before I had the chance to explore it fully.

"That's good, I guess." Casey shrugged.

"Yeah, I'm going over tomorrow to learn all the basic stuff, and then the program is going to start Monday after we're done class," I said. "You should meet Eric, the guy who runs the place. He's an Iraq vet. Talking to him is like talking to some kind of Jedi."

"Whoa," Casey said, getting up out of his chair. "He's going to teach you to do push-ups using only your mind?"

I rolled my eyes.

"Yes," I said. "Got to get my money's worth."

"Does that mean though you're going to stop drinking now?" he said, slipping on his shoes.

I still wasn't quite sure what going to a gym meant for me, I wanted to say yes, but I didn't want to make a promise I couldn't keep, so I shrugged.

"Ah," he mused. "Anyway, are you hungry?"

"I feel like I need something in my stomach and definitely more water," I said, looking at my hands.

"Alright, well, let's go to Burger King," Casey said, grabbing his keys. "I am starving, brother."

I reached for my phone, which was now fully charged, and saw that I had several messages from last night. Scrolling through, I noticed three missed texts from Sara.

SARA: SGsgsesrDG- That was from Cameron, he said he loves you.

SARA: Hello? He tried to call, but your phone is off.

SARA: Okay.

I hate how she spoke to me sometimes. She made it sound like I was purposely trying to ignore him, which wasn't true. *Why did she have to be like this?* I thought. It wasn't fair. She left me, and now she wants me to feel like an asshole all the time. I couldn't tell her my phone died because I was too drunk to plug it in because I knew she would make me feel like even more shit for missing Cameron's call. I texted back.

CODY: Sorry, I had to buy a new charger this morning. Mine broke. Tell Cameron that I love him.

I shoved my phone back in my pocket to follow Casey out the door, but before we could leave the apartment, it buzzed again.

SARA: Okay. I told him. Sorry about your charger.

I shook my head and threw the phone back into my pocket.

"What's that about?"

"Nothing. Cameron tried calling, and I missed it. Sara was pissed, so I told her my phone died because the charger was broken and I had to buy a new one."

Casey pushed open the back door to the apartment building as we walked down to his jeep. I kept mulling over why I still felt guilty lying to her. The large shadow from the building that was cast over the parking lot felt all-consuming.

"Super smooth," Casey said, unlocking the doors. "Won't she just check the bank account to see if you actually bought something?"

"Not my problem anymore, dude," I said, getting in. "She left me, and the money in the bank account is all my money. As long as Cameron is fed and rent is paid, I can do whatever I want with it." I put my feet up on the dashboard. "If she wants to complain about me spending money, she could get a job."

"I thought she worked in the tampon factory?" Casey said as the engine turned over.

"I'm not sure," I said, closing my eyes. "All I'm saying is we've been apart for a year, and she still sends me reminder texts about what and how to spend my money. It's bullshit."

"Fair enough," Casey said as we pulled out onto the city streets. "I think you've done alright though; I mean, look at us now. Living the dream and off to eat at one of the finest dining establishments in the city."

We both laughed. I could feel that the world was in flux. A large gaping unknown where the future was supposed to be. At least for the time being, here in the jeep, half hungover with a growling stomach, the unknown didn't seem as frightening.

Chapter Four:
The Wanderer

June 5th, 2017, 12:09am

"Where ya going, buckaroo?" Casey said, taking off his headphones and tossing them onto the desk.

I shrugged.

"Out, I think."

"I thought you said you were exhausted?"

"I am exhausted."

Casey picked up his phone and checked the time.

"You know it's almost midnight, right?"

"Yes, Casey, I know what time it is. I have a watch." I said, holding up my TIMEX and reached for the door handle,

"Wait!" he said, standing up. "Bars close in an hour, why not just drink here instead?"

Already in his pajamas, it was easy to see he wasn't interested in having to trek across Portland to go pick up his drunk brother again.

"I'm not going out to drink, dude."

"It's a Saturday night, and you're not going to drink? Are you buying drugs?"

"Bitch, am I bu…what?" I squinted. "No, you, asshat, I'm going for a walk."

"At midnight?"

"Yes."

"Oh, well, don't get stabbed. We have astronomy on Monday."

"Will do," I said, shutting the door behind me.

Stepping out into the empty streets, I was taken aback by how heavy the smell of humidity and exhaust sat in the air, making the world around me feel hazy. Streetlamps buzzed over red-bricked sidewalks. Massive bodies of brownstone buildings sighed over illuminated OPEN signs in shop windows. During the past week, the compulsion to wander had been slowly growing inside me like an angry seed. I needed to get out. Out of the apartment. Out of the gym. Out of my own aching skin. To quell the noise in my head. Taking a right down Park Street, I passed like a shadow by the Lafayette apartment building's half-empty parking lots. Wandering down into the soft orange haze of crooked streetlamps, it struck me that I had not been out like this in years. Not since Sara and I were together. Back in 2015, when I was still a sergeant of marines. Back when I had a purpose and a family slipping through my fingertips.

The idea to wander around aimlessly in the dark wasn't a habit that I had come up with on my own. Once, it was homework given to me by Amber, the psychologist provided by the base. Who Sara made me see when she figured out I wasn't the same man she waved goodbye to eight months ago. I had come back infected with a nameless disease that was slowly hollowing me out and I was the only one who couldn't see it. Closing my eyes, I could picture myself sitting back on a threadbare maroon couch in her borrowed office in the battalion headquarters.

"I haven't been able to sleep. I lie down in bed, and it's like the whole room gets louder, like it's slowly imploding, and I'm just trapped underneath the blanket." This was one of the few genuine things I actually told her in our weeks together. Most of the time, I was just trying to get in and out of her office without being seen. There was a taboo about seeing a psychologist even if everyone did it. Being caught signaled to the world, you weren't man enough to deal with your own problems. It was an embarrassment to your honor. However, I was having trouble sleeping in the last few weeks, and I was hoping that I could score a prescription of sleep meds out of the deal.

"Have you tried getting out at night? Doing something to tire yourself out?" Amber asked from a beat-up leather chair. She had just the faintest hint of wrinkles around her eyes and mouth that became more pronounced every time she would ask me questions. This bothered me for a reason I couldn't quite figure out. Maybe it was because those wrinkles made her look older, and her blonde hair seem whiter. As if talking to me could drain the life out of anyone.

I looked up at her from across the room and banged my aluminum cane between my tan boots. More than once, I wondered if the military had just hired actors to play psychologists.

"Don't think I'm the getting-out type," I said.

"Is it painful to move around?" she asked.

"No, it's just embarrassing mostly. I know the guys talk shit about me when I'm not looking."

"How long ago since you got hurt?"

"Uh… a year and a half?"

"What happened?"

"A fall," I said at last.

"Do you really need the cane to walk that much? I mean, don't take this the wrong way, but you look fine."

In all our time together, this was the first time she'd ever asked about the cane. I guess it was inevitable, but the "you look fine" comment burned. If only I was missing a limb or had scar tissue or a purple heart to wear, maybe people would stop telling me about how fine I looked. I didn't feel fine. I didn't feel fine every time I fell up or down the stairs, I didn't feel fine throwing up in the physical therapist's office, and I didn't feel fine when the base took my license away because I seized up behind the wheel of the car unable to keep track of all the movement.

"Sort of yeah," I said, "I get vertigo and dizzy spells a lot. The cane helps me keep my balance."

"You just get them at random?" she asked, writing something down on the giant yellow legal pad.

I was beginning to feel attacked, clutching the handle of my cane. I could feel the tone in my voice shift into a dull roar.

"Yes, that's why I have a cane. Are we going to talk about sleeping problems or not?" I cleared my throat and tried to calm myself down. I wasn't going to get pills if she thought I was an asshole. Collecting myself, I shifted my attitude and glanced at the clock on the wall. "Can you give me pills for sleeping? I need it." It seemed she got the hint about the cane and readjusted herself in the chair, bare skin squeaking on fake leather.

"Cody, I'm a psychologist, not a psychiatrist. I can't provide you with medication. You'll have to see your Battalion psychiatrist for that."

My heart dropped. A free psychologist was one thing, it was strictly off the books' help, but the battalion psychiatrist was a whole different animal. They were known as the wizards because they could make you disappear. One slip of the tongue, and you find yourself labeled mentally disturbed and medically discharged. Poof. Just like that. The wizard was used exclusively by guys who wanted out of their contracts, guys who couldn't hack four years in the military, so they claim some kind of mental health issue like it's a train ticket back to the civilian world. A trip to the wizard was the coward's way out.

"Fuck."

"Cody, I think you should give the walking a try. You don't have to go fast or far, but it would be good for you," she said, leaning back in her chair. "It will be time to yourself, meditate on things, and hopefully tire you out enough to get back to bed."

I hated the thought of someone one else knowing what was good for me. I could have come up with the idea of walking outside all on my own. It was hardly revolutionary; people have been doing it since the dawn of time. Even if it was a half-decent idea, accepting the advice was admitting that I couldn't take care of myself. I needed someone else to tell me how I would work best.

"It's February," I said, pointing back out the window to the lead-colored sky. "I'll freeze out there."

I didn't want to lose the chess-match.

"Grab a jacket, I'm sure the southern winter won't bite. Aren't you from Minnesota?"

"Maine," I corrected her. *How hard was it to keep the facts of the one patient you come here to see straight?* Had to be an actor. No psychologist can be this forgetful.

"Yes, of course. I'm sure if you can endure a Maine winter, you'll make it through a North Carolinian one." She smiled one last time and looked at the clock before shoving the legal pad back into her purse. "It seems we are out of time for now, but I will see you next Wednesday, yes?"

"Sure, Doc," I said, rocking myself off the couch. "See you then."

When I got home and told Sara about what the psychologist had suggested, she wasn't enthused. The relationship between us was already showing foundational fractures. Trust was one of the first things to slip under the surface of suspicion in the first few months since getting back. I had dedicated more time to my phone to escape the anxiety around me, which began to arouse what was at first benign suspicion. It all started out innocent enough. Sara would put on a movie, and I would get bored and text my friends, and she would ask me things like, "Who's that" or "What are you talking about?" over the coming weeks, it became an almost daily question.

She came to believe that my lack of interest in our love life was due to another woman. A reality that would eventually prove true. But not for the reasons she thought. I was frantically building a wall between her and me that I wasn't even conscious of. She made me paranoid and angry with simple things. Everyday things a wife does, like asking, "How was your day?" or "What do you want for

45

dinner?" felt more like an interrogation. I became convinced that she was always watching me.

"What's the point of me seeing a psychologist if I'm just going to ignore what she says?" I said, collapsing into the living room couch. Sara was sitting on the opposite end, crouched in the corner.

"I'm not saying ignore her. I'm saying I don't like the thought of you leaving in the middle of the night," she said, not even bothering to look at me.

"Fine. I'll just stop seeing the psychologist if you disagree with her advice."

"THAT'S NOT WHAT I'M SAYING!" Sara yelled, throwing her hands up in the air. Cameron, who was still a toddler, copied her from his highchair.

"SWAYING!" he shouted and broke down laughing. We both gave a quick and reluctant smile.

"Fine, walk, whatever, just don't get hurt. At least take a heavy jacket. It's cold outside."

On my first night out, I waited until after Sara went to sleep to leave the house. I felt like I was escaping from the dragon's lair and out into the cold. Moving along the sidewalk, I found nothing but silence among the rows of identical homes of base housing. It was an imposing silence that I had not anticipated. It made my stomach knot with both thrill and anxiety.

Taking a seat on a bench next to the empty playground, I took out a tangled pair of headphones and cranked the volume up on Brand New. As the music rose and fell, the pit in my stomach grew, making the moment feel heavier than it had before. Finally, I had a breakthrough that had eluded me my entire time in therapy. I wasn't the problem;

it was the world around me. Since coming home hurt, everyone from the former platoon commander all the way up our chain of command was trying to fuck me over. They were poisoning me from within, trying to take everything away from me. I hated them. All of them.

***

My aching feet took me out of my thoughts. My left hip throbbed in its socket, forcing me to take a seat on the granite steps of one of the historic condos on the road. I had only been off my cane for two months since moving to Portland, and my body was still adjusting. The luminescent numbers of my watch glowed underneath an ever-ticking second hand. It was thirty past midnight. Looking up towards thy sky, I noticed just beyond the limited reach of lamplight, the silver crescent of the moon was breaking free of the clouds.

Does Sara know I don't need a cane anymore?

The question came into my head uninvited and sat uncomfortably in my throat as I tried to swallow it. Why was that important? She was six hundred miles away in Pennsylvania, getting on with life, and I'm the last person she would be thinking about. Standing up, I pushed my fingers into my hip to calm the pain and continued on. My memory of those last few years is still jumbled up in my head. Fractured, incomplete, like a puzzle missing most of its pieces. Facts, assumptions, and rumors fused together into one narrative, with only a few pictures to fill in what I had lost. Photos of me working on a motorcycle I'd never ride, one of me alone at a bar, me drunk in a bed that wasn't mine. In each photo, a stranger wearing my skin gazed back at the lens with an empty smile and shiny eyes.

I began to sweat inside my jacket as I crossed into the heart of Portland's nightlife in the Old Port. Neon lights of closing bars and the few opened doors beckoned me to come in and have a drink. Inside *Fore Play Sports Pub,* the bar was empty save one lone man hunched over his phone with half a glass of dark ale. I felt my feet drifting towards the door, and I had to make a conscious effort to keep them on the sidewalk. However, they didn't carry me too far down the road before I found myself in the doorway of my favorite bar, *Old Port Tavern.* Pushing on the heavy wooden door, I made my way up the narrow stairs to the bar where rows of pool tables stood neglected. Taking in the sounds of Johnny Cash, who was singing over the speakers to nobody.

On a stack of milk crates, Krystal sat, ignoring the loud emptiness. There was an elegance in the way she sat. Her straight copper hair brushed to one side, adorned with glints of bronze and silver that illuminated the dark corner of the bar. It was as if she had been made for one painting and dropped into another.

"Hey, Mom," I said, startling her into a smile.

"Hey, sweetie!" she said, getting up and throwing her arms around me, "Are you okay? It's a bit late."

"I'm fine. Just out for a walk is all. Thought I would drop in and say hello." She motioned for me to take a seat on one of the tall chairs at the bar.

"Do you want something to drink? I got whiskey neat if you'd like, my treat."

My mouth watered, and I swallowed hard against temptation and, with some effort, managed to decline, "Thanks, Mum, but not tonight."

"Water it is then," she smiled. "So tell me, where are you walking to this late at night if you're not looking for a drink?"

"I'm not sure. I just didn't want to stay home, started feeling claustrophobic in my own head."

She stared past me with a faraway look as if I had triggered an unpleasant memory. "I get that."

I took a sip of my water. "Maybe I'll go spend the night on the beach?"

"That sounds like a wonderful idea," Krystal said, shaking herself out of whatever had been weighing her down.

"Really?"

"Yeah, why not? The ocean is lovely, and it is such a beautiful night out, who knows what magic you'll discover in the dark," she said, glancing dreamily over the counter and out one of the wide windows across the room.

"Sure, yeah, I think I'll do that. How's the night been here?"

"Quiet. You're the only person I've seen in the last hour and a half."

"Oh, that sucks. Why don't you go home early?"

"I could do that if no one else shows up in the next fifteen minutes," she said, looking at the neon rimmed clock on the wall that let us know it was thirty past midnight.

"Well, you close up, and I'm going to make my way down to the beach," I said, hopping out of my seat. "You deserve to get to bed early for once."

Krystal smiled, "So do you."

"No rest for the wicked, or something like that."

"You're not wicked," she laughed. An electric sensation crawled its way around my head, memories convulsing into an incoherent babble that locked me up.

"I would disagree."

"Honey," she said, putting a hand on my shoulder, "You're not wicked. Wicked people don't hurt after they hurt someone else, and that's the difference."

I shrugged silently.

"You have one of the biggest hearts of anyone I've ever met, and I've been around long enough to see it. One day you will too, but for now, go have a nice sit on the beach and listen to the ocean."

I hugged her before heading downstairs, "Thanks, ma, love you."

"Love you too. Be safe."

"I will."

I followed Fore Street down to India Street, which took you straight down to the paved biking trail that leads to the Eastern Prom. The bike path started at the end of the pier, where the CAT and Carnival Cruise docked to let off tourists. Hopping the small fence that separated the trail from the beach, I stepped onto a tumble of boulders that ran gently along the shoreline. Unlike the piers, the air off of the ocean here was salty and fresh. I felt invigorated and nestled myself into a comfortable spot between the rocks. The sky was clear, and the moon's cold reflection shimmered over the black water.

Pulling my knees to my chest, I tried to empty myself and allow the revelations to make themselves known. The ocean noise became an endless pulsing static as I slipped into a shallow meditation. Minutes passed. I waited, but my thoughts remained formless. I started to get irritated. The urge to get out of the house had been eating at me all week. Not a single revelation stirred. No magic. Sitting straight up, I exaggerated deep breaths out, making sure to drop my shoulders and relax my facial muscles. I tried one more time to sit and let the words come to me on the moon-soaked beach.

Why do I keep thinking about Sara anyway? Why does it matter? I thought. *Weren't there other things to think about?*

"Fucking god damn it," I muttered to myself. Opening my eyes, I laid down between the rocks admiring my failure. *I came out all this way for nothing.* A small fire of inadequacy was beginning to burn in my chest. The sound of the ocean chased it back down my veins and snuffed it out. *I guess I need the walk regardless.* If I wasn't going to get my epiphany, at least I had a nice place to lay my head for the night. Some people pay money to listen to the sound of the ocean before bed, but tonight I had the real deal right in front of me. Taking off my jacket, I laid it across me like a blanket. The rock underneath me was still cold, but I was able to convince myself that it would warm up the longer I lay on top of it.

A stiff breeze off the ocean swiped gently at my face. I stared into the multitude of blinking lights from the many islands across the bay. Pinpricks of red, green, and orange in the dark, going on and off like matches in the distance fighting the wind to stay lit. My eyes came to rest on a single buoy that flashed on the r eastern side of the island. The emerald green light making eyes at me from across the water.

I allowed myself to become hypnotized by its monotonous flashing. Watching the long trail of green that came and went on the water. In the stillness of my thoughts, the phrase, *Cody turned out alright in the end*, erupted to the surface, breaking the silence. I tilted my head in confusion at my own thoughts, *Gatsby?*

Cody turned out alright at the end. The words throbbed.

I sat up against the rock and pulled my jacket over my shoulders. Consciously I finished the next sentence. *It was what preyed on Cody, what foul dust floated in the wake of his dreams.* Much like Gatsby, I had been the architect of my own undoing. But in my story, I was Daisy, the car, the gun, and that foul dust all wrapped up into one ugly package. My heart stung with the truth I had known since the beginning began to fill me up. *I had been the one who pushed Sara away. I had fought against a life that allowed me to be a husband and father in favor of being alone with my own swirling misery.* Somewhere deep inside, I knew that I had wanted to be alone. No, I *deserved* to be alone. But, now, I wasn't so sure.

Even after the doctors diagnosed the brain injury, it did nothing to stop the shadow that was consuming my body, *that foul dust.* When Sara finally left me, I felt a sense of relief. I was free and far away to become the black hole that I was turning into. *Cody turned out alright in the end.* Is there such a thing for people like me? For people that break the hearts and souls of the ones that loved them the most? Who balances the checkbooks? Maybe there is no turning out alright in the end. There is only an end. A year ago, I would have been content with the knowledge of life fading to black, but ever since moving to the city, that had changed. These people who had started to come into my life, Eric, Courtney, and all the others I was getting to know, had cast strange magic over me. I had started to enjoy being a part of Portland. I didn't want it to end. They made me happy, and I only started to be okay with that.

CRACK
SNAP

Sharp and familiar noises pierced the night, and I instinctively got low, pressing myself into the boulders, trying to make myself as small of a target as possible. Pulsing blood rushed into my limbs and ears, erasing the last moment from my mind. I fell into autopilot, surveying where the gunshots had come from. I slowed my breathing and took deep, long breaths. *I don't have a gun.* Everything was static. I was a deer in the headlights.

CRACK

The noise brought me back to reality.

On the far end of the beach, I could see three dark male figures in the sand staggering around near the water's edge. They were too far away to make out any concrete details. I squeezed my pocket for my phone and carefully slid it out, making sure to keep it face down on the off chance that the glowing screen would give away my position. I watched one of the men drop down to the sand for a moment before getting up and running away.

The red flash of a firecracker blasted low across the sand, and then I could hear the three men start to laugh and holler, putting their arms around one another. A deep sense of relief washed over me.

It was just fireworks.

I wiped away the beads of sweat that had begun to form on the sides of my face and took a deep breath, shaking my head. A year later and I'm still reacting like I never took the uniform off. Still jumping at imaginary gunshots. I clicked the side of my watch, and the indigo light revealed that it was ten to two. Looking back towards the island, I had lost the green light somewhere along the shoreline. Shaking the sand off my jacket, I stood up in defeat.

"Almost had it."

Chapter Five:
Codessious

June 7th, 2017, 12:35pm

"Fuck, man, this is really kicking my ass," I said, reaching for my cup of water. "Deadlifting blows." Eric was sitting off to the side, watching my form, his heavily tattooed arms folded over his chest. He shook his head and walked over to me.

"I know it can be frustrating, bro, but I need you to watch your language," he said gently. My face contorted into an unsubtle mix of annoyance and confusion, which Eric picked up on straight away. "Look," he said, pointing to the post across from us. Bold silver letters painted on the white wall reading CODE OF CONDUCT with five simple rules on the membership form I had signed a few weeks earlier.

"Rule number three, watch your language," he said.

"Sorry," I said, stripping weights off the bar.

"No, bro, it's totally fine," he said, making his way around me to the small kitchen that was just opposite the work out space. "You know why I have that rule?" he said, walking into the kitchen area to make another pot of coffee.

"To keep things family-friendly?"

Eric just laughed, the kind of laugh that parents make when their kid tells them that rain is just God taking a pee.

"Well, sorta," he said, throwing grounds into the filter. "Part of it is because, yes, I have all sorts of people in here, and you don't want to say something that will make them feel uncomfortable." Eric turned the machine on, and steaming water began to hiss loudly as coffee began to drip into the pot. He walked out of the kitchen, passed me over to one of the three pillars that supported the upstairs balcony. He pointed at the word "Truth" glowing in the morning sunlight.

"Each time we use negative language, we fill ourselves with that negativity," he said, looking at me. "When we use words that are meant to express hate or anger, it rubs off on us, gets us thinking in negative terms."

In all my life, I had never once thought of swearing as a harmful activity. I wasn't entirely buying into the philosophy of it.

"Yeah, but what if something sucks?"

"You can think it sucks, but instead of saying, 'this is kicking my ass,' say, 'Next week, this will be easier because I'm getting stronger.'" I had to stop my eyes from rolling and remember that was his gym, and so I found there was no point in arguing.

"Alright, will do, boss," I said halfheartedly. Eric smiled and patted me on the shoulder.

"That's the spirit, bro," he laughed, going back into the kitchen. "You want a cup of coffee?"

"Sure, man, I appreciate it." I could feel the heat radiating off my skin, I ached for water, but I didn't have it in me to turn down free coffee. While Eric grabbed two mugs from the rack above the coffee pot, I busied myself with cleaning up the rest of my mess. Putting one of the steel plates away, I caught myself staring out of the large bay windows that looked out onto the sidewalk. I could see my second-story apartment, my blue beanbag pushed up against the glass. It was strange to think just a year and a half ago, I had a bed and a wife to share it with. I shook the thought from my head.

"Here you go," Eric said, handing me a black cup of steaming coffee. It burned gently in my hand, but I didn't say anything. "So, I don't know if you know this, but in a few weeks, Optimal Self is having a little adventure day at a place called Tumbledown Mountain, a little bit of hiking, hanging out with friends, I think you should come." A crackle of electricity raced through my skin as I was seized by a familiar fear. My heart began to race, and I could feel my hands go numb, forgetting about the coffee burning its way through my palm.

"Uh," I couldn't think of the words to say. It wasn't that I didn't want to go, but I had no idea where this place was, how many people were going, what the weather was, there were too many unknowns. Things my brain couldn't calculate. Too many threats to keep track of.

"Cody?" Eric asked. "You okay?"

I swallowed some coffee, "I'm sorry, man, it's my brain, you know?" The words came tumbling out. "I want to go, I mean, I really do, but when I think about it, my head turns to static when there are too many unknowns in a plan," I looked around and whispered, "I get scared, I can't help it." Eric didn't say anything. He just stood there for a few seconds, looking out onto the sidewalk, watching the morning commuters make their way to work. I was beginning to think I had pissed him off.

"Sorry, I shouldn't have said that." I shook my head, my lungs filling with a mix of shame and disappointment.

"No, Cody, you should be able to tell me these things," he said, at last. "We're both veterans, and I know the feelings you're talking about." Taking a seat on the bench, he cleared his throat and looked up at me. "When I got done in Iraq and came home, I was so…angry, so paranoid about everything, I felt like I never wanted to leave my house. I spent a lot of time drinking just to deal with the thoughts of going out there into the world. It was like everyone out there was an enemy trying to destroy me. I felt like I was always on patrol, always ready for a fight…I needed to be, or else the world was going to get me when I wasn't looking."

This is me, I thought. These were my words coming out of his mouth.

"How did you fix it?"

"I fought it. The military didn't make us warriors, Cody. It was something we were already born with. So, I did what warriors do, I fought it." The air around us seemed to hum in low steady noise that I could feel on my skin as he spoke, "I hit back by finding a new purpose for my life, a new mission," he said, looking up at the slow spinning fan above us. "Every warrior needs a mission. We protect, we help, and we fight. It's in our DNA. Without a purpose, we get dragged down into those dark places."

"How do I find my mission?" I asked. The whole moment was so surreal to me.

"You got to listen to your spirit and search it out. I can't tell you what Cody needs to do. I only know what Eric is supposed to do."

My heart sank.

"I don't think I have a mission then. The only people I cared about, I ended up hurting. I mean bad. That's why I'm here and not with my family anymore."

"No, bro, you can't think like that. Whatever happened in your past drove you here, to this moment. This chance to really figure it out."

"People like me don't deserve to figure things out." The words bit back on my tongue as soon as I said them.

"Everyone deserves a second chance," he said, standing up. "Especially people who have looked into themselves and accepted responsibility for their actions. No matter how bad it tore them up."

In the silence, I didn't realize that I had tears forming in the corners of my eyes.

"I knew it from the moment you walked into the gym that you were a warrior, you're going to figure it out, and I'm going to help you. Come to the hike in a few weeks."

"Alright, I'm in."

Eric pumped his fist into the air and yelled out across the empty gym, "Mighty Codessious! Conquering the great MOUNTAIN OF TUMBLE DOWN!" We both shared a laugh.

"Thank you, Eric, seriously," I said, looking at him. "I've been stuck for a hot minute, the therapists are helpful and everything, but it just...it feels different coming from someone who has actually been there, you know?"

"No problem, I'm glad to help. After all, this gym is my mission right now, and to help whoever comes through those doors to become better versions of themselves."

Crossing the street back to my apartment, I kept flipping Eric's words over in my head. I truly wanted to believe in the sentiment that everyone deserved a second chance. But my mind dragged me back to two years ago, waking up in an empty bed, my phone missing. I was still drunk walking down the hallway to see Sara sitting on the couch with tears in her eyes. We *need to talk*. One of the handful of memories I had left of our marriage. There is still a lot I didn't remember about the final days of our marriage, but I'll never forget the look of devastation on her face when she discovered that even after I promised Amie was a one-time thing, that I was lying. There were new names. New texts. She cried, and I remember feeling nothing. Absolutely empty on the inside. Sara didn't understand what she had done wrong, but that was just it. She didn't do anything wrong. I was so tired of living in a lie that I reached out for a chance at momentary happiness with strangers.

"Why are you doing this?" her voice cracked. Tears falling onto the dirty couch.

"I don't know," I shrugged. "Guess I just wanted to."

Inside, the AC was on full blast, making me shiver. Casey was at his computer watching something on YouTube. I tapped him on the shoulder on my way to the kitchen to let him know I was home.

"How was the gym?" he asked, spinning around in his chair.

"It was alright," I shrugged, reaching into the closet for a clean shirt.

Casey frowned.

"You're not going to take a shower before school?" he said with disapproval. Grabbing some paper towels off the roll, I wiped the sweat off my forehead and out of my armpits.

"There. All showered."

"You're vile."

"I was born that way," I said, throwing on some deodorant and one of the many plain grey shirts we owned.

"Fair enough," Casey said, yawning, getting up from his desk. I made my way back to my side of the room, putting on clean pants and jamming astronomy books into my backpack. Sitting on the windowsill, I glanced at the sidewalk below where people busied themselves with the starting day. Eric's words floated through my head before I shook them out.

"You want to go for coffee before class?"

Casey groaned.

"That means driving," he said, shoulders slumping.

"We drive to class anyway?"

"But…effort," he said, throwing himself back down in his chair. Casey could be just as easily equal parts lazy as he was helpful. The inconsistency was one of the few things about him that got under my skin. Luckily, I knew how to motivate him.

"BOY, IF YOU DON'T GET YOUR ASS OUTTA THAT CHAIR!" I yelled, pelting him with dirty socks from the basket. Cowering, he threw his hands up to block the incoming assault, but it did no good.

"ALRIGHT, ALRIGHT!" he said, screaming in defeat. "Let's go to Dunkin." Casey put his shoes on when my phone vibrated in my pocket. I was still laughing when I looked down to see who was texting me. My heart dropped.

SARA: *Hey. Don't forget, I'm coming up with Cameron at the end of the month. Do we need to get our own hotel?*

I hesitated before writing back.

The apartment is a studio, so maybe? You two could have my Yogibo if you want.

"OKAY," was all she wrote back. I took a deep breath and put my phone back in my pocket. Things between us for the last year could be described as professional, but every time she messaged me, my heart still twinged in my chest. I was ready to be told what a piece of shit I am, even though she'd never said a word about me since we separated.

"Are you ready yet?" I asked, looking up from my phone.

"Yeah, let's go," Casey said, grabbing his backpack and shoving his keys into his pocket.

On the way down the stairs, I knew that I didn't have what it took to tell Sara she needed to get a hotel room. It was a nauseating weakness, but I knew I also didn't have the money to put both of them up in a hotel room for the weekend, so I latched onto that excuse and made myself feel better about telling Casey that they would be staying in the room with us.

"In the studio?" he asked, pushing open the door onto the streets.

"Yeah, we'll figure something out. I'll sleep on the floor if I have to."

"When are they coming?"

"Uhh, 20th through the 24th?" I said, looking down at the bricks.

Casey shrugged. "If you think that's going to work out, then sure."

I said nothing as we crossed the road. I didn't know if anything was going to work out.

Chapter Six:
Oh

June 17th, 2017, 4:03am

A light rain was beating on the window when I woke up. The room was still dark, and I could hear Casey gently snoring on the air mattress across the room. I reached for my phone and was blinded by the screen, which read 4:03 June 17th. *Fuck*, I thought, rolling into my blankets. There was no point in getting up. Sara and Cameron would be here in a few days, and the stress was starting to get to me. I didn't know why. I mean, this wasn't the first time that Sara had come to visit me. In fact, when I was still living at my grandma's house, all three of us shared a room, so what was it that made me so nervous over a year later? I imagined her frowning when I told her that she would have to sleep on the floor like the rest of us because we didn't have room for an actual bed. I thought of her frowning disapproval of the state of our almost always empty fridge or the crowded desk we did our work on. All of these seemingly inconsequential things were growing into a checklist of failures waiting to be picked apart.

I stretched and looked in the dark for my cat, Mighty but saw nothing. He was probably still sleeping by Casey or on top of the fridge. Outside, the streetlights illuminated the darkened windows of Optimal Self, which were blotted with raindrops. Wrapping myself up in the blanket, I was struck with the thought, Sara has never been to Portland. The lightbulb went off in my head as I lay in bed smiling, THAT'S WHAT IT IS! Neither she nor Cameron had ever been in the city before, and not knowing how they're going to like it must be keeping me up. It had nothing to do with my apartment. It was not knowing if she would like the city! The pit in my stomach disappeared, if only for a moment, before queasily making its return. I closed my eyes, shaking my head. *Of course, they've been to Portland, dumbass, nice try.* I tried to press myself back into sleep. A chainsaw like snore ripped from Casey's side of the room, followed by the sound of junk hitting the floor. I opened my eyes to see Mighty sitting on the edge of the desk nervously, looking down into the dark where Casey was sleeping.

"Me too, buddy," I whispered across the room. "Me too."

The next time I woke up, it was because the sun was in my face. I sat up and looked out of the window. The street and sidewalks were still stained by the rain, but the sky was clear over the darkened brick buildings. Casey was still snoring, but it felt like a good idea to go take a walk. It was still early, but I knew the city was very much awake. I got dressed in silence and closed the door behind me, making sure to leave a sticky note that said I was out, just in case. Outside there was a slight chill in the air, but the summer weather was still comfortable enough for shorts, even this early in the morning. Across the street Optimal Self was open. Through the window, I noticed a woman sweating on the treadmill, and through the open door, I could see Eric with a coffee cup in hand, giving directions to some poor soul in the squat rack. I smiled and turned down the sidewalk towards the coffee shop.

Coffee by Design was one of the main drains on my wallet. They opened early, and their mind-bending delicious locally roasted coffee had elevated my once non-discerning palate into a snobbish one. After living in the city for a month, I could no longer stomach the burnt taste of Dunkin Donuts' coffee and refused to surrender my hard-earned money to them any longer. From now on, only the finest bean water would do for me. The fact that Dunkin was also a ten-minute walk farther down the road probably had something to do with it. Pulling open the door, I was surprised to see that there wasn't a line at the counter, which was odd for eight in the morning.

"Hey, what can, I get for you?" the bearded barista asked, leaning over the counter.

"Can I get a large black coffee, no cream or sugar?" I asked. Anything other than black coffee wasn't coffee to me.

"Sure, coming right up."

I gave the man the old smile and nod, thanking him under my breath as he handed me my drink. One bonus of drinking straight black coffee, there was no wait time between the order and being on your way. Meanwhile, some poor soul is still waiting nervously about making it to work on time after ordering their large decaf Jamaican blend with half liquid sugar, one pump of hazel, two pumps of coconut, with a splash of foam and extra non-dairy creamer on the side. I took a seat in the window, which looked directly ornately carved brick and sandstone building that dominated my whole view. It had Greco-Roman faces carved high in the sandstone. The un-approving stares of stoic men judged silently of those down on the sidewalk going about their day. Above the archway were the words BAXTER BUILDING, which hints at the building's long-forgotten past. Below the arch was the much more confusing letters V/A. When I first arrived in Portland, I thought the words stood for Veterans Affairs, but since learned it was only an advertising agency.

The Department of Veteran Affairs had a notorious reputation before I became a civilian. It was a dirty word that conjured up images of endless waiting lines, dying in hospital beds, and misappropriated funds. It didn't help that the Head of the Department had been hired and fired twice because of controversy. I prepared myself to die silently among the hordes of forgotten in the waiting room. Although when I was finally processed at Togus up in Augusta, the whole transition was unexpectedly smooth. I remember back in late 2016, just a month after I had left, when my grandfather took me the hour drive north to the facility. He stopped the truck in the parking lot and pointed to an old brick building with ornate windows.

"Your great grandfather, my father, spent six months on the top floor there recovering from back surgery," he said, flicking the ash from his cigarette out the window. "I used to play in the fields over yonder whenever mother would come to take us for a visit."

I stared out the window, squeezing the walking cane between my legs. "That's really cool Grandpa, I had no idea."

"Oh yes, and before that, my great grandfather, Wilbur Fisk Mower, who was in the Civil War, would come here and give speeches, back when it was a home for disabled veterans of the Grand Republic," he said, turning into the parking lot.

"Wilbur died young, didn't he?" I asked, trying to remember his entry in the family history book. Wilbur's story was long. He went into the army as a private and left as a lieutenant. He fought in Gettysburg and Vicksburg (against my grandma's folk), was shot twice, captured twice, and escaped both times. I can remember being in awe reading his story, but I couldn't figure out how it ended.

"Wilbur died when he was fifty-two, I believe, of melancholy."

"Melancholy?" Across time and space, I felt my spirit rise in my chest and hitch itself to the memory of Wilbur. I wonder if he, too, couldn't stand waking up in a body that was nothing more than a vehicle to experience the numbness of day-to-day living.

"Yeah, melancholy, it's what the old-timers used to call depression," Grandpa said, reaching up in the visor and taking out three scratch tickets.

"I know what it means, Grandpa," I said, opening the door.

"Then why'd you ask?" he said, grabbing his lucky coin from above the ashtray.

"Nothing, I didn't mean to."

"Oh, well...ALRIGHT...when you get done, I'll be right here," he said, smiling.

"Thanks, Grandpa, love you!" I said, shutting the door behind me. I had no idea that Togus had been such a family affair. Walking through the sliding glass door, I was continuing the one-hundred-and-forty-year tradition of Mowers in military hospitals, dying of melancholy.

***

Staring over my half-empty coffee cup, I began to grow restless with my window seat. The crowds of people were slowly making their way into the shop, which started to make the anxiety build in every heartbeat. I collected myself and waved at the barista as I stepped back out onto the sidewalk. The rising sun was starting to evaporate all traces of last night's rain, which you could feel sticking to your skin. I wasn't ready to walk back to the apartment yet, so I decided to head into *Optimal Self*, even though I wasn't due to work out for a while. On the second-floor balcony was a small table next to the massage chair that Eric had pointed out, which felt like the place to be.

"Cody!" Eric said, as soon as I walked through the door. "Morning, bro, how are you doing?" He was standing in the small kitchen, coffee in hand, wearing a sweat-soaked grey Optimal Self shirt.

I gave a fleeting smile. "Good, man, I'm just going to go sit upstairs next to the massage chairs if that's alright?"

"Of course. You alright, man? I rarely see you this early."

I shrugged. It was impossible to keep emotions hidden from this guy.

"You take a seat and relax, and we'll talk in a bit?"

Over the last few weeks, Eric had a way of recognizing when I was getting negatively in my own head whenever I was working out. I'm sure years of helping people and his personal journey through the dark place had helped inform him of the different signs and symptoms to look out for whenever someone was slipping, but to me, his abilities bordered on the supernatural. Just like the first meeting I had with Eric, something had compelled me to trust him, and so far, it had felt like the right thing to do.

"Yeah, that's fine. I could use a quick chat," I said, making my way up the stairs. I took a seat at the table and put my face back over my coffee, but by now, it was lukewarm, and instead of steam, I just saw my blotched reflection in the bean water. I hadn't rehearsed anything I would talk to Eric about, so I just hoped not to make an ass out of myself when he came up to talk.

I didn't have to wait long. My face was still staring into my cup when I heard the chair scrape next to me.

"You find any answers in there?" Eric laughed, taking a seat.

"I wish, man."

"Coffee is the answer to everything, bro. If you want something fresh, the pot is on downstairs."

"I appreciate it," I said, gathering my thoughts.

"Of course, so what's on your mind? You stay away from the drink?" he asked, taking a sip of coffee.

"Actually, yes. I was even tempted pretty bad the other day while I was out walking on Fore Street, but I talked myself out of it."

"Heck yeah! Proud of you, Cody. I know that can be really tough. That takes a lot of courage."

My face flushed with a mix of pride and embarrassment. I wasn't used to people saying encouraging things to me like that. The moment quickly passed and was replaced with a sickly feeling that bubbled down in my stomach. Even though Eric said I was courageous, I felt like a fraud.

"Thanks," I said, clearing my throat. "Actually, um, so Sara is bringing Cameron up in a few days. I haven't seen them since November, and I'll be honest, I'm fucking petrified of her coming here. It's a bad feeling. I know it's irrational, but it's keeping me up at night." I took a breath, my heart beating faster as if I had said too much.

"I see," he said.

"It's not your problem, man, I'm sorry, I just needed to say something to someone," my hands were shaking from embarrassment and regret. *How many times was I going to tell this poor guy my problems?* I thought to myself, in a fit of growing anger at my inability to keep my feelings in my own head. I searched Eric's body language for signs of internal cringe, but he just sat there, nodding his head as if he were putting puzzle pieces together.

"What? No, bro, don't apologize. That's what friends are for," he said, moving the long strand of his ponytail from off his shoulder.

Did he just call himself my friend? Alright, I'll take that, I thought, trying to process his words. I don't think I had ever had someone just proclaim to be my friend so boldly before. But he seemed like the kind of guy you'd want on your side.

"Okay, I appreciate that."

"I think I got it figured out, though. You've built a whole new life here in Portland, with school, the gym, and everything all on your own. So, this is the first she and your son has seen you since living with your grandma…"

I thought about this, trying to wave off a creeping sense of skepticism that was crawling in between my ribs. A part of me wanted whatever he was about to say to be wildly inaccurate, so I could hold on to the heavy emotions that made me feel like a person with depth.

"Okay?" I said, wondering if I missed the revelation.

"So, maybe what you're feeling is like…you've built something separate, a whole new life without her, in the city and by yourself, and that can leave you feeling pretty vulnerable to judgment. Not just about you, but like, is this a place for Cameron and such," he finished.

"Oh," was all I could say. The answer he gave was so pointed and accurate that it made me feel like a moron for not seeing what was right in front of my own face.

"Does that feel close to home at all?" he asked, his brown eyes searching for offense. "If I got something wrong, forgive me, man, that's just all I could pick up."

"Oh shit, no, I mean 'oh' as in you're so correct, and I couldn't see what was right there in front of me," I said, taking a sip of my cold coffee. "I can't believe I couldn't see that…in the final years of our marriage, when things were really cold, it was nothing but judgment and suspicion from both sides. We could be sitting on the same couch, not looking at each other, but you could feel the hate looking over your shoulder. I didn't think I still carried that with me."

"It is the simple things that can be the hardest to see," he said, crossing his arms and staring down at the gym below. "It's okay to need help finding that sometimes, but remember whoever you were sitting on that couch, that isn't you now. You got to give yourself some credit, and even if

Sara judges you or says what you've built is no good, it's good for you right now, and that is what is important. The better person you learn to be, I'm sure the better father you'll learn to be...I don't have kids or anything, but how could it not make you better?"

The tears began to sting my eyes, but I wiped them away and swallowed the wave back down. Not once. Not until this very moment had I ever considered that the person in the past was a wholly separate identity. That part of me lingered on my skin, no matter how many times I tried to scrub it away.

"Do you really believe that?" I asked, staring up at the lights to keep the tears in. "You really believe you can be two different people like that?"

"People evolve and change all the time. Even the cells in your body change completely every six months. Physically you're a whole new person. And the fact that you are even here in this chair talking to me is proof that you aren't the same person that was in grandma's house or on that couch. You're getting better bro, believe that. It's okay."

I chewed on his words for a minute, nodding silently. Like most of the things that Eric told me, they were ideas that gave me hope, but it was hope I kept at a distance. I couldn't comprehend a way of existence that was separated from the mistakes of the past. All the therapy I had been to over the last three years revolved around coming to terms with mistakes, but no therapist had ever mentioned anything about the person who made those mistakes as "someone else." It was an idea that I wanted to believe in, but I don't know if my inner being could rationalize the irresponsibility of moving on so carelessly. Mistakes are meant to be felt. That's what keeps you from doing it again. You earned that pain…I won that black smudge on my soul, and it became a part of me, a reminder of how low I could go.

"Yeah, maybe," I said, finishing my coffee.

"Just think about it, alright?" he said, standing up. "I'll see you a little later for training, okay?"

"For sure, I'm just going to sit here for a minute if that's cool?"

"Take your time," Eric said, putting a hand on my shoulder, "with everything."

"Thank you. I really appreciate it."

"Yeah, man," he said, walking away.

I closed my eyes and imagined what it would have felt like to leave my sins in the past. My lungs tingled as I practice the forbidden rite of forgiveness, pulling my spirit from my body to walk around weightlessly in my imagination. It felt dangerous and uncomfortable, but even in my fantasy, the feeling didn't last long, and I was snapped back into my body. Clearing my throat, I made my way back across the street to the apartment. Casey was still asleep on the air mattress when I opened the door, making sure to shut it quietly behind me. Taking a seat in my chair, I threw my feet up on the desk and stared at the wall. A growing number of papers had begun to be tacked to the wall. The syllabus for all five of my summer classes was above the printer in a neat row. A drawing of SpongeBob that Cameron had mailed to me and a printed picture of Odin towered above it all, staring down with his all-knowing one-eyed gaze.

The All-Father was undoubtedly a complex character in Norse paganism. The wisest of all the gods, he pursued knowledge at all costs, including crossing lines of certain taboos. In one story, he was chaffed by Loki for the year he spent living as a woman to learn the art of female magic of seidr, which was forbidden to men. How did he get over doing something so extreme? Why is it that the Gods never seemed bothered by their mistakes for too long? Maybe that sort of clarity of consciousness came with being divinity and that I was not. I looked back towards the window and sighed, *would be nice, though,* I thought. Over in the corner, the squeaking of the air mattress broke the silence as Casey sat up blurred eyed.

"Good morning, star shine," I said. "The Earth says, *helllooo.*"

Casey grunted and waved his hand in acknowledgment. Standing up, his twig legs popped as he walked towards the bathroom. Watching Casey get up in the morning was like watching someone in a nursing home. There was a lot of grunting and body cracking, and no matter what, he always looked like he never got enough sleep even if he had been assed out for eleven hours.

"Good morning, brother," he said, with his voice coated in sleep.

"Morning," I said, spinning toward him in my chair.

"I had this weird dream that I was in some kind of robot world. I was the only human left, and people were treating me like a mix between royalty and a zoo animal."

"Do you think it means anything?" I asked, unsure of what to say to such a random recollection.

He shrugged.

"Maybe it means that the human race is doomed?" I thought out loud.

"No, that can't be it because they were happy to see me," he said, bringing my coffee over to me.

"Do you think that who you were in the past is a whole separate person from who you are now?" I asked nonchalantly.

Casey stared at me and blinked before shaking his head.

"Brother, it is too fucking early to comprehend philosophy right now."

"Yeah, that's cool and all, but do you think it's possible?" I said, turning back towards my laptop as Casey came and took a seat next to me on his side of the desk.

"I haven't even had my coffee yet," he said, throwing his head back in his chair.

"You have it in your hand, so I don't know what you're bitching about," I said, taking a sip of mine.

"Fair enough," he said. "Uhh, yeah, I think it's possible."

"Really?"

"Well, yeah, sure," he said, "I mean, are you the same person you were when you were fifteen? Your motivations change, your wants and needs are different, and yeah, isn't that what defines a person?"

I sat there absolutely fascinated and blown away by Casey's answer. My younger brother was the most rational person that I have ever known, and I think part of the whole reason I asked him was that I expected to get the 'people never change' speech. Some kind of ground my cynicism could stand on. But to hear him agreeing with the more eccentric ideas of Eric was an exciting moment. It made me wonder if behind that forever calm exterior if he had asked himself the way I was now.

"Why do you ask?" he said, leaning back in his seat. "You dealing with something?"

"No, I just heard it somewhere, and I forgot to ask what you thought about it."

"Ah, I see," he said. I couldn't tell if he believed me or not, but if he didn't, he certainly didn't give anything away, "That's fair, what do you think about it?"

"I'm not sure if I'm honest. At first, I was really against the idea, but it may be a legit thing."

Casey shrugged and logged into his computer. "Well, at any rate, we both have to write up our lab report for astronomy because it's due next class. You want to write it up, and I'll just plug in the numbers?"

"Sure, I already wrote it up, actually," I said, pulling up the report on Word. "I'll just email it to you."

"How do you get this work done so fast?"

"I don't know, man, having things on my list gives me a panic attack. It's like I can't even breathe knowing I have a deadline to meet."

"Oof." He laughed.

"I blame the Marine Corps," I said, stretching. The muscles in my back were thankful.

Casey grunted, and we slipped into the silence of schoolwork. I enjoyed our conversations, even if I never told Casey directly, but I don't think I had to. He knew.

"One more thing," he said, looking up from his screen.

"Yeah?"

"You sure you want Sara to stay here in the apartment?"

"Yeah, I think that will be alright."

"Just checking," he said, going back to his work.

"I know."

Though I didn't say anything, a quiet feeling of unease was building up inside my chest. A part of me was gearing up for what was sure to be Sara's critical analysis of how I lived here in the city. It wasn't going to be good enough. I still wasn't good enough. I felt as though I needed to prepare myself for the impending arguments that were sure to surface in the wake of her visit.

Later that afternoon, I began to clean up the apartment a little for Sara's arrival. I still didn't know enough about Portland to take them on a full tour of the city, but I knew where the Kid's Museum was, and the ocean was only a short walk away. Tomorrow was Sara's birthday. It was already too late to send her a card, and with all the time and space between us, I had no clue what I would even pick up as a gift. Folding my clothes, I tucked them into the corner between the wall and my bookshelf. Sending her a text would have to do.

Chapter Seven: Expectations

June 22nd, 2017, Noon

"They're in the city," I said, throwing my phone on to the desk.

"Does she know where the apartment is?"

"No, they're at the Spring Street parking garage, so I'll have to get them," I said, slipping on my shoes when it dawned on me that I was not prepared for her arrival. I had known for almost two weeks, she was going to be staying, but it felt like a far off, and distant thing, so remote that to even think about it was a waste of time.

"Are you regretting letting them stay in the studio?" Casey asked, walking into the kitchen for some water.

"No," I said. "Honestly, I couldn't afford to put them up in a hotel for the week, so this is saving me money."

"That's not what I asked, but okay."

Grabbing my keys off the desk, I shoved them in my pocket before opening the door. "I don't know, man, I really just want to get this over with."

"I can come with you if you want."

"No, that's fine. I can do this."

Before I had a chance to breathe, I was already outside. The summer cruise ships brought with them masses of tourists, who moved lazily across the redbrick sidewalks. Crossing the road, I was tempted to pop into *Optimal Self* and let Eric know my son and my ex were here, but I didn't want to keep Sara and Cameron waiting. *Ex?* I thought *that didn't sound right*. Walking towards the parking garage, I caught a strong smell of weed, and it occurred to me that I hadn't labeled Sara an "ex" or anything else. We had been legally separated for over a year, but we never got around to filing paperwork for the divorce. Now that she was here, I wasn't sure how I would introduce her to my friends or if that was even something I should do.

The parking garage wasn't far from the apartment. I hadn't even begun to sweat under the summer sun before I was standing in front of the four-story concrete garage.

"Shit," I said, reaching into my empty pocket. I had left my phone on the desk. I felt as if things were already off to a bad start for me, now that I was going to have to search four floors of the garage to find them. The sound of my worn-out Converse sneakers slapping cement echoed off the walls as I went searching for her red Prius. After much huffing and puffing down the wide concrete steps, I spotted it nervously tucked away in between two trucks on the third floor. The figure of a woman sat behind the windshield. The lines of her face filled out as I got closer like an apparition forming from old memories, which was becoming flesh and bone. When our eyes met for the first time through the glass, the world constricted inside my head. Feelings of dispassionate indifference melted away into an inky sea of vague curiosity.

"DADDY!" Cameron's voice broke through the haze. I caught a glimpse of his rose gold hair in the backseat before, in a flash, he was outside, throwing his tiny arms around me. Kneeling down, I squeezed him gently. Since I'd last seen him the previous November, he already looked taller, his frame more robust, built for exploration. My body swelled with both pain and pride as I held him on the cold concrete.

"Hey buddy," I smiled, "You've gotten so big!"

"Yeah, I know," he said in a hurry. Letting go of me, he went back to the car and pulled out a crushed Marine Corps cover that I used to wear and threw it on his head.

"Look, now we're both in the army!" he said.

"Marine Corps, but yeah, sure, dude," I said. My body felt like it was floating, and I wished that this moment would stretch on beyond the fleeting reality it was grounded in. Dusting my knees off, I noticed Sara was still rigidly glued to the front seat as if she too was somewhere else. I took a step back so she could open the door while Cameron hurried around the car, pulling and tugging on a suitcase that was wedged firmly in the back seat.

Dressed all in black, she emerged from the car. Like Cameron, she, too, had changed since November. Her eyes had grown dull, framed by a look of exhaustion that didn't belong to her. Even her body didn't seem to belong to her. It moved heavily and without purpose as she walked towards the trunk in silence. I squinted for a moment, trying to match up the draconian voice I was used to on the phone with this stranger standing in front of me, but I struggled to make the connection.

"Hey," I said with some effort.

"Hey," she said back in a whisper.

"How was the ride up?" I asked, shifting my gaze from her to the trunk.

"It was fine," she said, "Long."

"Oh," I said.

"Yeah."

"You want to grab something to eat or something?"

She shrugged her shoulders.

"You've straightened your hair. It looks nice."

"Thanks."

"Hey, Dad, where do you live?" Cameron asked.

"Just up the road," I said, glad for the change of topic.

"I've never seen a city like this, except in New York!" he said, his bright green eyes flashing.

"Well, Portland is smaller than New York, but there is some cool stuff to go and see," I said.

As Cameron and I talked, Sara began to take out two small suitcases from the trunk.

"Do you need help getting anything?" I asked.

"No," she said. I couldn't understand why she was so quiet. We weren't five minutes into being around one another and it already felt as if she didn't want to be here.

"Okay, let's go then."

When we finally finished climbing the concrete steps to the door of my apartment, my heart tightened. This was the first time Sara was going to see just how Casey and I were living. The thought made me irrationally nervous, but as I pushed open the door, I knew there was no going back. As they wandered into our tiny studio, Cameron was immediately drawn to the large bay window where I slept. Pressing his face to the glass, he looked down at the sidewalk below, transfixed by the comings and goings of the city. On the other hand, Sara was silent as she had been, gliding from the doorway to my empty chair like a ghost.

"Hello, ma'am," Casey said, getting up from his chair.

"Hello, sir," she said with a repressed smile.

Casey began talking with her about school and filled her in on what had happened to him since he left the navy. The door shut behind me, and I wheeled Sara's suitcase over to my side of the desk, not knowing quite what to do with myself. The moment was surreal and far out of place from the memories carried inside me. There were no dirty looks, no murmurs of resentment, nothing which hinted at the arguments I had readied myself for, just a muted calm.

The day passed quickly in our overcrowded apartment. Though the excitement of the city was just a step out the door, Sara was too tired after her eight-hour drive to go out for dinner, though Cameron wanted to uncover all the secrets of this uncharted city of brick.

"We can order Taco Escobar for dinner?" I suggested, wheeling around in my chair. Sara was sitting with Cameron on the windowsill, trying to keep him from knocking on the glass and waving at the people below, and she shrugged.

"I don't care," she said, eyes fixed on some imaginary hole in the carpet.

"Uh, okay," I said, not knowing what to make of her passivity. For the last five hours, she hadn't engaged with anyone beyond short, polite conversation or acknowledged anyone else in the studio except for when she would courteously rearrange herself around the apartment if she was in your way of getting to the bathroom. It was like having an unsettling piece of living furniture.

"Yeah, let's get tacos!" Cameron said, jumping onto the floor.

"Casey, tacos sound good then?" I asked.

"Uh, I mean if you want to get them," he said, not looking up from his computer.

"You mean you're not going to eat them?" I questioned.

"I'm just not hungry," he said, still watching a video.

"Sara, do you want tacos, or you don't care?" The indecision in the room was nauseating, but I wasn't going to spend forty dollars on food just to have it picked at.

"I'm not really hungry either," she said, looking back out the window.

"Great," I said, rolling my eyes.

"Can I have two tacos?" Cameron said, pulling tiny toy cars out of his backpack.

"I don't think anyone wants them, bud."

"Oh," he frowned, running the cars along the carpet.

"Well, I guess we can go to *Joe's* and get something small for everyone," I said at last, "then maybe tomorrow we can go try some of the restaurants."

"Okay," Sara whispered.

"Come on, Casey," I said, patting him heavy on the shoulder, "Come help me carry food back."

Joe's Corner Store was a late-night staple for Casey and me. It was one of the few places in the city that stayed open until 11pm that wasn't a bar, which made it the perfect place to stock up on food or energy drinks when you weren't ready to sleep. They also had a full-service kitchen that made surprisingly good chicken wings and cheeseburgers.

The bright fluorescent lights gleamed off the polished floors, illuminating the dark sidewalk as I pulled open the door, letting some of the AC out into the humid summer night. It was almost ten, and the place was practically deserted. Jeannie, the immovable fixture of the night shift, waved a wrinkled hand at us as we filed in.

"Hello, boys," she said.

"Hey," we said in unison.

Staring at the side cooler, Casey pushed up his glasses before fumbling through the kitchen food that was set out for the night.

"Do you think she'll eat a chicken sandwich?" he asked.

"No, dude. Sara and Cameron are both vegetarian," I said.

"Oh, well, that's…okay." Casey knelt down to look at the salads on the bottom shelf, his knees making an audible pop. Bending down, I whispered to him,

"Does Sara seem weird to you?"

"What do you mean?" he whispered back.

"Like, I don't know, she's been really quiet and shit since she got here, I don't know what to do with that. To be honest, I was expecting some sort of fight or argument, but instead, it's like talking to a wall."

"Is that a bad thing?" he asked. "Also, why are you whispering?"

I grabbed two veggie wraps and tucked them into my arms, along with a cold burger from the top shelf. "Sorry," I said, "I don't know why I felt the need to whisper."

"What? Is she going to hear you from the apartment?" Casey said, walking down to the drink coolers.

"Who knows, man? Back before we split up, it was like she had eyes and ears everywhere," I said, looking around the empty store.

"Ew, one of those situations?" he said with a frown.

"Yeah, but I mean, I kinda deserved some of it," I said, "I'm afraid of saying something and then getting stuck in an argument or talking about the past." We collected our drinks and made our way towards Jeannie.

"Talk about something else then. You're in school, going to the gym, and all that shit," he said. "Why don't you ask Sara about what she's doing?"

I felt queasy at the thought of asking her about herself. I knew a large part of how she was doing was directly a result of me. That question felt like the key to opening Pandora's Box, and I wanted to last the week without feeling like I needed to crawl into a bottle of Jack Daniels to drown myself in.

"You boys all set?" Jeannie asked, taking our food.

"Yes, ma'am," I said.

"That's a lot of food you got tonight. Friends over or something?" she asked, smiling.

"My son and…" My brain locked up. It was the moment I knew would come eventually. "His mom is here visiting for the week." The words tumbled out of my mouth like loose stones.

"Sounds like fun, sweetie. It'll be $23.55," she said, placing everything into a bag. I ran my debit card into the machine and gave her one last courtesy nod. "You boys have a goodnight now."

"You too," we said in unison again before walking back out into the night.

Just before we reached the apartment door, Casey motioned for me to stop, and he dug out a can of Grizzly Wintergreen pouches. Setting his bag down on the sidewalk, he threw two pouches into his mouth before handing me the can.

"Would thou likest some nicotine, brother?" he asked.

"It's not alcohol, so it's not technically going back on my word to Eric," I said, setting down my bag down next to his.

"Yep, plus it is a good way to relax," he said, spitting into the road. I took the can and needlessly packed the tin as if it was loose leaf. Old habits, I suppose. After a few slaps of the tin, I pressed two pouches into the soft of my lip.

"You know I used to dip all the time, back in my first enlistment," I said, spitting off the curb. "Then one day, I came home from work, and Sara had dumped all my dip into the trash and told me to quit."

"Oof," Casey said as he laughed, "I would have cried. Dip is all we had back on the ship."

"The navy be like that," I said. "The Marine Corps didn't care. In fact, I think the more shit other than blood you had in your system, the easier it was to exist."

"Maybe I chose the wrong branch," Casey said, spitting back out into the road as the car rolled through, its headlights catching the bay window of *Optimal Self*. My eyes fixated on OS, and an unusual feeling of guilt settled over me like a fine layer of dust. Though I enjoyed the nicotine rush, I couldn't help but feel that I was making some sort of mistake, though unable to nail down the reason. Spitting the pouches out into the gutter, I picked up my bag and stretched.

"Let's not keep them waiting,"

"I'll be up in a second."

Walking into the lobby, I stared at my feet before turning up the stairs. *Why did I feel wrong about tobacco?* It was such a stupid thing to feel bad over. I've done a lot worse with my body, by comparison, so what was the big deal? *Weird*, I thought.

"Alright, who wants what?" I said, pushing through the door. Sara was sitting at my desk while Cameron sat on my beanbag in the window.

"It doesn't matter. You remembered we're vegetarian, right?" Sara said.

"Yes? I only lived with you for six years," I said, trying to make a joke out of it. Out of the corner of my eye, I could see Casey cringe. Putting the bag on the floor, I handed both Sara and Cameron their food. "Here you are."

Sara's face recoiled, "Did you start doing dip again? Your breath smells like that wintergreen crap."

"Uh, no," I lied.

"Right," she said, getting out of the chair and took a seat next to Cameron. "Guess we'll eat on the floor since there isn't any table."

"Ma'am, we're men of little luxuries in this house," Casey cut in.

"I can see that."

Chapter Eight:
Who Are We Now?

June 29th, 2017, 8:30am

We carried on through the week like a captainless ship, drifting bumping through the current of the days, listlessly and without bearing. Though Cameron seemed to take no notice of the tension between Sara and me, I found it increasingly hard to breathe around her. For the most part, she said nothing and followed us around like a walking portrait of the American Gothic, her face frozen in a constant state of unenthusiastic wonder at the life I had created in Portland. I tried to be upbeat for Cameron's sake, but it was a hard front to keep up when you feel like you're being met with contempt at every turn.

As the sun rose on their last day in the city, I was glad that my usual routine of schoolwork, the gym, and going to my coffee shops in the morning wasn't too far away. Everyone was still sleeping when I started to get dressed for the gym, but Sara lifted her head up from the floor as I turned the handle.

"Where are you going?" she asked, squinting from the shadows.

"Oh, I was going to workout early, so we would have more time to do other stuff before you guys leave," I whispered.

"Okay," she said, laying back down. "You look good, by the way, you look healthy again."

This was the first time in the whole week she's been here that she had given me anything resembling a compliment. I was completely caught off guard.

"Thanks," I said at last. "That's the plan."

"Well, bye," she said in a whisper.

"Bye," I said.

Carrying myself across the street in the morning chill, I found it hard to concentrate on settling into my workout. Even as I smiled and waved to Eric, my thoughts were circling Sara's compliment. It was subtle, but it shifted the entire tone of her visit. It was an unusually quiet workout for me as I retreated into my head, caught in the twilight of the moment. As I finished up a set of lackluster bench presses, Eric came over to me, coffee cup in hand.

"You alright, bro?" he asked, his tattooed arms tensing in the morning light.

"I'm okay, yeah," I said, wiping sweat off on to my shirt. "Today is Sara and Cameron's last day in the city."

"I'm sure they had a great time. I saw you guys walking out of the building a few times. Man does your kid look like you." Eric laughed.

"No, saying it was the mailman on this one," I said, cringing at my inability to small talk.

"Yeah," Eric paused. "Is that what has you all silent over here?"

"No." I took a seat on the end of the bench and looked up at the ceiling, trying to order my thoughts. "Sara told me that I looked good this morning, and I don't know what it means."

A puzzled look dragged itself across Eric's face. "It could mean she's noticed that you're looking better?"

"It can't be that simple," I said with a quickness. "It can't be that simple."

"Uh, why not? Sometimes people just mean what they mean."

"Do they, though?"

"Yeah, people have been known to do that."

"I don't know. It's the first nice thing she's said to me since being here."

"Listen, someone gave you a compliment, you've been working hard over the last month, so just accept it and feel good," he said, shaking his head. "Not everything needs to mean something else."

I sighed and nodded my head as if I understood. "Alright, yeah, sure, thanks, man."

As he turned to leave, Eric looked back at me, pointing a finger. "This Sunday, Tumbledown Mountain, be here at six am."

"Wouldn't miss it for the world."

"I know you wouldn't," he said, making his way up the stairs to the office.

When I got back from the gym, Cameron was sitting on the edge of Casey's deflating air mattress, trying to take his socks off while Sara sat in the window, browsing her phone.

"How was the gym?" she asked.

"Uh, it was good," I said. "You find anything to do for y'alls last day in the big city?"

Sara stood up and grabbed some clothes out of her suitcase, "I thought we could go to the narrow-gauge railroad museum and just walk around?"

"Sounds good. You want some coffee?"

Casey, who was still bleary-eyed from being awake before eleven, just nodded. Cameron continued his assault on his feet.

Sara moved past me in a blur as saying something I couldn't catch. A long string of mumbled words followed her into the bathroom.

I looked back at Casey and whispered, "What she'd say?" But he just shrugged. By the time Sara had finished her shower and was ready to go, it was just past ten. Out in the noise and heat of June, the sidewalks were filled with tourists, meandering lazily under old arched windows and brownstone buildings.

"Are there always so many people?" Cameron asked as I held his hand. We were making our way down Exchange Street for a late breakfast at the famous Holy Donut.

"Not always," I said, looking down at him, "only during the summer when tourist season hits."

"Are we tourists?"

"I don't know," Sara cut in. Unlike the rest of the week, today, Sara walked next to me. If anyone had seen us, they would have said we looked suspiciously like a family. Not only was she not skulking around two steps behind, but she also dressed differently. Her hair was straightened down past her shoulders, she wore jeans instead of black leggings, and even though it was hard to tell, I thought I saw a hint of make-up in her eyes.

"No, buddy, as long as I'm here, you're not tourists," I said at last.

After donuts, we took a short walk down to the bike path on the water where the old narrow-gauge station was.

"Where does the train go?" Cameron asked.

"Nowhere now. In the early 19th century, these thin trains carried things from as far away as Boston, all the way into Canada. However, as technology advanced, the small trains like these ones were left behind to become tourist destinations," I said, trying to remember the bits I had heard.

Cameron didn't seem to care about all of that, though, once we got into the museum. The place was adorned with cast iron train parts, thick glassed lanterns, and just about every wall had a dusty black and white photo of some various pieces of locomotive history. The big draw was the museum centerpiece, a narrow-gauge locomotive with an attached coal car, painstakingly restored to become a jungle gym for children.

Every thirty seconds, it was, "Dad! Dad!" or "Mom! Take a picture of me!!" and Sara and I followed him around from room to room, filling our phones with a menagerie of silly faces, horribly fake smiles, and poses on antiques that were probably meant to stay free from tiny hands. The three of us danced around the cramped museum for over an hour, laughing, and making jokes that echoed off brass whistles, glass cases filled with musty conductor hats, and squinting faces of more reserved tourists. Exhausted and hungry, we were making our way out through the gift shop when a silver-haired woman behind the counter offered us three tickets for a ten-minute ride on the only functioning narrow gauge train left in the state, only forty-five dollars.

With a lighter wallet, we made our way into the stiff heat of the afternoon, Cameron holding both our hands, unable to contain his joy at the sight of the waiting train. It was a small but impressive locomotive painted deep forest green, with lacquered black trim that caught sunlight and wonder in our five-year old's eyes. There was nothing eye-catching about the hard, thin, wooden benches we sat on inside the train cars. We scrunched together in the front of the car, facing the ocean. Sara sat next to me, her thighs pressing into mine as the train lurched to life. The smell of coal smoke and ocean salt filled the small car. Through the glass, the train moved scarcely faster than the people walking on the bike path next to us. Closing my eyes, it felt as though, if only for a moment, I was someone else, somewhere else. Caught up in the twilight of the moment, my hand fell from the back of the stiff bench to Sara's soft leg.

She smiled.

"Can we move here?" Cameron asked, taking a break from window, gazing. The question shattered the fragile nostalgia and hung throbbing in the air like a wound. Sara and I looked at each other, and I quietly removed my hand from her thigh to grab Cameron's hands.

"Well, bud," I said, trying not to kill the joy in his little world, "I have to go to school at the big university, which takes up a lot of time. So maybe when I'm finished school, we can talk about you and mom coming up here, okay?"

I could see the gears in his head moving as he turned over my proposition and gave an unsatisfactory "Okay" before looking back out of the window and at the ocean that was slowly rolling by. Sara and I didn't say anything to each other until well after the train ride, and we had started walking back into the city when she asked me where we could get some ice cream. The rest of the day was a whirlwind of souvenir shopping, food sampling, and watching Cameron enjoy being a kid. Up until this visit, I hadn't allowed myself to enjoy being a father. It was a joy I felt I didn't deserve, but over the week, something shifted in me, and it was no longer something I had control of, and as night swept through the streets of Portland, I found myself mourning their departure.

As we lay down to sleep that night on the floor, I scooped my son in my arms, not knowing when the next time I would get to hold him would be. I don't know how long I had been dreaming before I was startled awake by a loud whisper in my ear.

"Hey," Sara said.

I opened my eyes. The walls of the apartment were faintly lit by the streetlights breaking through one of the half-shaded windows, and I could make out Sara's silhouette hovering so close to my face, I could feel her body heat radiating against my cheek.

"Is everything okay?" I whispered, sitting up.

"Yeah," she said, "Come here." In the dark, I watched her shadow move silently across the floor towards the bathroom. Standing up in a dim glow, I knew what was about to happen. I knew why she was calling me into the bathroom, and something deep in my bones told me not to follow. But I hadn't been with anyone since before things went bad with us, almost two years, and that was all it took.

As the door shut and locked behind me, I convinced myself that maybe, somehow, this would change something.

Sara pulled me close and kissed my face. Her warm hands moved across my skin, grabbing, squeezing, searching greedily around my waistband. My heart began beating in quick, heavy beats as I lifted the shirt over her head and threw it on the floor. We kissed and groped at one another, hands full of warm skin, familiar, and close. Our naked legs danced lustful circles in the dark until I was lying back on the cold tile floor. She kissed her way down my chest, her hair dragging along my torso like a long brushstroke. My mind became a roar of static as I felt the heat of her mouth send chills up my body, and I became entirely lost in forgotten sensations.

I was so caught up in the moment, I hadn't noticed that she had changed positions and was finally on top of me. With adjusted eyes, I could see she was using the sink to steady herself as she rocked back and forth. Slowly, I became aware of how warm and wet the insides of my legs were. The smell of sex and sweat began to turn fetid. The anesthesia of nostalgia rapidly started to deteriorate in the dark, and to the soundtrack of Sara's soft moans, I found myself trapped. My legs twitched involuntarily to get away, but a strong wind of guilt kept still.

When I finally came, I was relieved that it was over. Instead of pulling herself off me, Sara lay on top of me like a blanket, hot, sweating, the smell of her breath repulsive. Sensing something was wrong, she rolled onto her side, and the cold air wrapped me up, and I shivered. "What's wrong?" she whispered.

For a moment, I was silent. She wanted an answer to something that I hadn't even figured out myself. "Nothing," I said in the dark.

"It doesn't seem like nothing," she said. With those words, I think she realized that whatever fragile thing we built today had just shattered across the floor of my apartment.

I grunted.

"Did it not feel good?" her question was laced with hurt. If this had been two years ago, I would have lied and told her it was fine. But lying just to protect her feelings was something I no longer had in me.

"It felt different."

"Different how?" she asked.

"I don't know yet," I said, looking for sweatpants.

A long silence swallowed the bathroom as we moved around each other, searching for clothes to cover our nakedness.

"Can you leave, please, so I can go the bathroom?" Sara whispered.

"Yeah," I said. Closing the door behind me, I walked back to the makeshift bed on the floor. Cameron was still fast asleep, his hands stretched far above his head as if he was flying far away from here. I lay next to him, putting my finger in one of his open hands, just like I used to when he was a baby, though this time he didn't close his fingers around mine. I smiled for a moment and heard the toilet flush. Sara said nothing as she got under the blanket, turning her back towards me.

The alarm on Sara's phone woke me up the next morning as the bronze rays of sunlight peeked through the window. Casey was still sleeping when we left the apartment to make our way to the parking garage. Sara hadn't spoken a word to me besides a hushed "thank you" as I opened the doors for her. Outside it was colder than it had been in the last week, and I kept my hands in my pockets as we took the concrete steps to the Prius. After loading the suitcases into the car, Cameron gave me one last long hug before climbing into his car seat while Sara leaned on her door, staring at the ground.

Cameron said, "I love you, Dad," buckling himself in.

"I love you too, buddy," I said, brushing his red hair back, "You be good for Mom, alright?"

"I will," he said with a smile. "Next time we come up, can we stay in Portland?" My heart dropped, and I could see Sara shift uncomfortably out of the corner of my eye.

"We'll see," was all I could think to say. I shut the door and turned to Sara. She folded her arm and spoke to me without looking.

"You know it didn't have to be like this," she said.

"How else was it supposed to be?" I asked, already exhausted with this conversation.

"If you never...if...I." Her eyes searched oil stains on the concrete for answers, but I already had them.

"I can't take back the past, Sara, and I'm not going to live there either," I said, leaning back on the car door. "For what it's worth to you, I'm sorry. I really am."

In one quick motion, she tore her brown eyes from the ground and fixed them on me. "Am I just supposed to accept that you have this whole new life in Portland? Where are Cameron and I even supposed to fit in your life now?"

I could hear the mix of anger and heartbreak in her voice, which I hadn't heard since we split. It was the same tone she had used when she caught me lying through my teeth. But, this time, I had no reason to lie. There was nothing to try and hide. When my words came out, they came out clean, filled with a truth which neither of us had spoken in a long time.

"Sara," I said, "I did some ugly things to you and our family, with the lies and the cheating. With the distance. I was an asshole. But, I'm not that person anymore, and I'm ashamed that I was. However, I can't go back to being in a place where that will be the only picture of me. I can't live, waking up every morning like I owe you something. I will always love you and Cameron. Always. And I will try to be the best father I know how to be. But I don't know where you and I will be."

She looked at me and didn't say anything for a minute. "Okay."

That was all she said as she moved past me and got in the car. As she started the car, she rolled down the window to say something, but I got words in first.

"I don't think there will be an us if that day never comes," I said.

"What day?" she asked in a whisper.

"The day where we can legitimately move on," I said, "If not, then Cameron deserves to see his parents with people that love them. He needs that example."

"Okay," she said again. I could tell that she had so much more to say, but I knew she wouldn't let it go. "I'll text you when we cross into Vermont."

"Be safe," I said.

"Sure."

The car slowly began to roll its way down the ramp. I waved, kept waving even as the car disappeared around the corner. A sense of mourning of our past relationship washed over me in a heavy wave. For the first time, it came without the pain and anger I had felt towards her. As I kept waving at nothing, hot tears welled up in the corners of my eyes and escaped down my cheeks onto the concrete. Something inside of me had shifted, and I felt lighter, cleaner. I wiped my eyes, cleared my throat, and began walking down into the noise of the morning.

Chapter Nine:
Tumbledown

June 30th, 2017, 9:45am

"It wasn't an explosion," I said, looking out the window of Eric's jeep. Small beads of rain had begun forming on the glass, falling from the ash grey clouds above. I had been working with Eric for a little over a month, and with each passing day, I'd come to value our friendship. However, I'd never told him what had caused my injury, and the idea that he thought I was some kind of war hero like himself began to creep into my head. I felt like a fraud.

"Huh?" he said, barely even looking over as he scanned the road for the right exit.

"My injury, it wasn't an explosion," I mumbled this time, "Just thought you should know." A high-pitched ring buzzed in the back of my ears as my heartbeat hard as I sat waiting for the inevitable.

Looking over at me, he shrugged. "Well, that's good, bro, explosions are a nasty business, and I'm glad you weren't in one."

I paused. I don't think he knew what I was trying to say. "What I mean is, I didn't get hurt in combat. It wasn't even that traumatic. I made some mistakes, had some accidents…I didn't do anything heroic."

An unreadable silence filled the void between his seat and mine.

"I see…"

"Just in case you thought I'd actually done something," I said, cutting him off in a nervous outburst. "I don't want you to think I'm someone I'm not."

"Cody, I don't care if you were in combat or out of combat when you got injured."

The ringing in my ears grew louder as I sat, unable to look at him. I was beginning to regret agreeing to this hike.

"Injuries, combat, none of that stuff makes you a hero or even a warrior. That all started years ago. Being a warrior is something you're born with. That drive to protect the weak, to defend those who can't do it themselves, you're born with that, it's that simple.

"As for being heroic. Bro, when you signed the dotted line and told this country that its people were worth defending, no matter what the cost, that's heroic." Putting his hand on my shoulder, he looked over at me, "You, my friend, are a warrior. Who has already committed some heroic deeds."

"No," I said, looking back down at my feet, "I've hurt people, Eric."

"Do you want to talk about it?" Eric asked gently. Out of the corner of my eye, I could see him grabbing the GPS to get a better look. "We got some time before we get to the mountain. I'm ready for the story."

Pressing my hands together in my lap, I became aware of the humming of the road under the tires, and I tried to find where to start in methodical rumbling.

"It was an accident, or rather, I think it was a series of accidents," I said. "Personally, I couldn't tell you which one caused it...or maybe it's everything all at once?"

Eric nodded, keeping his eyes on the road. Even though he was wearing a long sleeve shirt, I could see the muscles tense as he squeezed the steering wheel, turning his knuckles white.

"I hit my head on a cliff in Korea. There was a scuba incident where I nearly drowned in Okinawa. I only remember darkness, and not to mention a few drunken fights in the barracks," I said, squeezing my hands. "It was all dumb, stupid kid stuff."

"I hear you, but I still don't see anything to be ashamed of," Eric said, flipping on the blinker as we reached our exit. "Accidents happen, and the last part sounds like normal grunt things."

"That's what I told myself. At least for a while."

"I take it your chain of command didn't see it that way?"

"No, I don't think they took me seriously," I said.

"Unless it's an arm or a leg missing, it's right back to work. I know how it is," he said, glancing over at me.

"Things were happening inside my head, shortly after the fall in Korea," I said, my heart still beating heavy. I had never gotten this far in telling my story, not even with the psychiatrist. I had shackled myself with silence. Closing myself off from people, believing that if I kept my stories to myself, no one could hurt me with the truth of my own failures. For a while, that worked, but after living in

103

Portland and meeting all these people…I wanted something more than safety. I tried to connect. Sure, I had made friends, but there was always this shame keeping any real connection at arms distance. I needed to take the chance. It was time to try.

"I didn't notice it, actually. It was my friends and my wife," I said. "I started detaching from people. I found myself getting angry a lot. As that deployment marched on, I found myself in a lot of trouble because I couldn't help myself from snapping at people, especially superiors. I guess that was giving them reason enough to hate me."

"I see."

"On my off time, I'd find myself just wanting to be alone. I knew it wasn't like me, but even when Sara would call, I would just ignore it and lie in my bed."

"That's never good," Eric said. "That sounds like a brain injury to me."

"Yeah, it just got worse and worse. You know when I got home. After seven months, fuck, man, I'll never forget. Sara had waited for me for so long. I saw her in the crowd, waiting for us to get off the buses, she must have been so excited and happy, but you know what I felt?"

"Hm?"

"I felt absolutely nothing. No joy. No excitement. I wasn't even nervous. My brain was so hyper-focused on the shit I needed to do. Her first words to me were, 'I love you,' and you know what I told her? 'Okay, I need to go get my bags.'" I squeezed my hands so hard, my nails bit into my palms, dotting them with deep crescent indentations. "I mean, who the fuck does that?"

104

I didn't know what to expect. I wanted to give Eric room to interrupt with his sage wisdom, but it was too late, the words were flowing out of me, and I couldn't push them back in.

"I should have known, right there, day one, that I needed to go see someone. That wasn't me. I love my wife. I love my son. They told us that there may be some adjustment issues, coming back off from deployment, but it just never stopped. On top of all that, I was starting to get vertigo attacks. They would get so bad, Sara would have to take me to the hospital. I felt like I was being swallowed up from the inside out by some shadow."

The hum of the road and gentle tapping of the rain-filled the brief gaps of silence between my breaths.

"I got to a point mentally, where I couldn't feel anything. Fuck. I mean, Sara went out of her way to surprise me for my birthday with a trip to DC to visit all the museums and shit. I didn't even say thank you. I don't think I even smiled the whole time. My vertigo attacks started to become so bad that they sent me to see a doctor after like seven months. Where finally, they discovered that there was something wrong with my brain. I ended up on a cane to help me keep balance. By then, it was too late for anything. My chain of command was disgusted with me. They moved me from my unit to an administrative one. They kept me away from people. Fuck, if I wasn't reminded how much of a piece of shit I was every day by some staff NCO or some fucking officer. Then I would come home to a family I felt like a stranger in…I wanted to die."

I hated to hear myself rambling, but the aching in my chest kept pushing me forward.

"One of the few marines that still gave a shit about me, Jackson, he was trying to keep me from going over the edge the best way he knew how. Which meant that I started spending more time away at the bars or having him over at the house. I guess being the son of an outlaw biker, it was all he knew. He led, and I followed. All the while, what was really important was slipping farther and farther away."

"Then October came," I whispered, "It had been eight months of this hollow existence. Every day felt like one eternity dragging into the next. I was ready to end it. Then I made a new friend. Her name was Amie." I shook my head. "That was a mistake. I met her at a house party that Jackson brought me to. The house was Amie and her husband, David's. David used to be in my platoon before they sent me away."

I looked over to study Eric's reaction, but he remained as still as he was when I started this story.

"I never cared for any of the party stuff, but it got me out of being around Sara, which just depressed me. Anyway, it was your usual shit show. Guys were snorting cocaine and Xanax, chugging beer. That sort of thing. Like always, Jackson would go inside and do his thing, and I would grab a beer and nurse it away from everyone else."

"So why were you there?" Eric asked.

"I don't know, man. Like I said, Jackson was just trying to help, but honestly, I couldn't tell you anything beyond that. I was an empty shell just bumping along."

"Alright, sorry to interrupt, I'm listening," he said, as we took another left out into the countryside. The rain was beginning to wane, but the clouds still loomed out in the cold.

"Anyway, yeah, Amie," I let out a long exhale, "You know, for someone who plays such a big role in all this, I can't remember her face. In my memories, all I can see are still images of the curves in her face and the electric red of dyed hair." I shrugged. "I couldn't even tell you what her voice sounded like, despite all of our conversations. How sad is that?"

"It's not uncommon for memories to blur with a TBI," Eric said. "Trust me, there is some stuff I'm still trying to figure out."

"That makes sense, I guess."

"Did you guys do something you weren't supposed to at the party?"

"No," I said, "Well, I didn't. About halfway through the night, I was sitting on the couch waiting to go home. I couldn't find Jackson anywhere. It was almost two in the morning, and I was tired. So I grabbed my cane and headed towards the door. That's when Amie stopped me and asked for my number to make sure I got home okay. So yeah, I gave it to her, but as I stepped outside, she ran her hands along my face and tried to bring me in for a kiss. But I shook her away and left."

"Noble of you," Eric said.

"Hardly," I said, "I didn't stop her because of Sara or my marriage. I stopped her because it made my heart race. Because for a brief moment, I felt something beyond the gaping emptiness, and I couldn't handle it."

"Did you tell Sara?"

"Yes, but no. When I got home, I was so tired I just flopped into bed and passed out. I guess Amie had been buzzing my phone. I didn't hear it, but Sara woke up. Amie sent me a long ass apology text for trying to kiss me, and it was all I heard out of Sara for the next three days."

"They always find out, don't they?"

"Yeah, well, she started telling me I needed to block her number, that I wasn't allowed to go out with Jackson anymore. On and on, treating me like a child. Looking back, it was good advice, but I just remembered being so angry. She was treating me like everyone else had since I got hurt. Like an incompetent child."

Squeezing my hands, I took another breath. "I remember starting an argument with Sara. I knew something nasty would get her to leave the house, and I guess it worked because I found myself alone upstairs. I made the bed. Smoothed out all the wrinkles and sat up against the headboard. I reached into my nightstand and pulled out my .308. You know, man, I was just…so happy to end it."

Reenacting the action in my seat, I brought my hand to the side of my head. "Even though it has been two years, I can still feel how cold the barrel was pressed into my temple. I had read that if you're going to kill yourself, blow through your temples because it's the thinnest part of the skull. I take my last breath and squeeze. I rocked back the finger gun to my head. Clunk. Nothing."

"A sign," Eric said in his eternal optimism, which I ignored.

"I start taking the whole thing apart. And found out it was a dud round. I replace it, get ready to pull the trigger again, and BAM, my phone goes off. It was Amie calling. I didn't want my last act on Earth to be ignoring someone, so I answered. She started going on about how she was sorry and how she didn't want to ruin having a friendship with me because I seemed like such a great person, and I ended up putting the gun away."

"I see what happened. She was the sign."

"Yeah, she was the sign," I said, drumming on the window. "I thought she was an angel sent to save me from myself."

"So, you cheated?"

"No, worse than that. I fell in love. God, it sounds so stupid now. How could we have been in love?" I said with a laugh. "Over the next few months, we talked and leaned into one another. She wasn't an angel. Just a twenty-year-old, far from home and in a life married to a man she didn't understand. We were just people made of sand, collapsing in on each other. How could that have ever been real?"

Sitting back in my seat, I turned my head towards Eric and made eye contact with him for the first time. Despite all he had heard, he remained calm, and though I searched for hints of disgust in the corners of his face to validate my fears, I found none. Only a soothing calm that invited me to wash myself of the stains which had up until this moment felt more like tattoos than smudges.

"Yeah, we got close. Real close. We talked every day. About life, our pasts, our future, music, books…In those conversations, I felt as though I could see a part of me coming back to life. I smiled more. I lived to wake up just to talk to her. Maybe I was going to make it after all," I said, shaking my head. "We lasted from October to March before it ended. She was over one night with friends at my house watching some TV, and I was half asleep with my head in her lap when Sara came home."

"Ah."

"In five months, that's the closest we had ever been physically, and the last time I would see her. But not the last time I would hear about her. Sara talked to her husband about everything, and they treated us the way high school parents treat rebellious teenagers. They teamed up and banned us from communicating. Blocked our numbers, and fuck man. I had felt as though Sara had taken away my only lifeline. I began to spiral."

"It makes sense."

"Over the next year, I start getting med boarded out of the Corps. Sara and I tried moving in with our friend Jackson in a new house off base to try to save our relationship, but it was too late at that point. It all fell apart. Sara and I were roommates. Nothing more. I had made more relationships outside our marriage, trying to get back that feeling I had with Amie. Each scheme getting found out. Each time it hurt Sara less and less. Shit, Jackson and I fell apart too. He got this girlfriend, who was also a marine, that would come to stay at the house. She would get drunk. Yell. She was even suicidal in our closet once. The final straw is when our neighbors complained that she was piss drunk on our lawn, like actual piss. Pissing at two in the afternoon on our lawn with a PBR in hand. We kicked them out."

"This was the best friend, right?" Eric asked. "The Jackson guy?"

"Yeah, we had been best friends for almost two years, and he took that boot as an act of betrayal. He sold my motorcycle, and, huh, he told David that I fucked Amie. You know, at first, I thought it was a joke until David started blowing up my phone with death threats. Tried to brush it

110

off. But in a plot twist, it turns out Amie is the one that told him that we fucked."

"Did you?"

"No. But at this point, who would believe me? I knew Amie wanted out of her marriage. Maybe this was her way of getting back at him. Anyway, I found myself abandoned by my wife, betrayed by Amie, fucked over my best friends, and now David trying to kill me. Not to mention the Marine Corps treating me like a liability. I just broke down. I was too tired to kill myself. Too tired to scheme. Too tired. Spent a lot of nights wishing David would just blow my brains out already. But it never came."

I was exhausted. I hadn't talked for so long straight in my life. My body was fine, but my brain felt cramped and dehydrated. "When I was finally retired out, it came as no shock to me that Sara asked me to leave. In fact, just two days after my retirement, I found myself once again packing up all my shit, except this time I was going to Maine to live with my gram, and Sara was staying with her mom."

"And now you're in Portland."

"Yep, and now I'm here," I said. "So, bringing it back around, I'm not a warrior or a hero. I'm a selfish cheater and a coward at my worst and a poor imitation of a human being at my best."

"So that's it, huh?"

"Yeah."

"No, I mean *that's it*? That's why you think you're not worthy of love or redemption? Because you got hurt and made some mistakes?"

111

"They were pretty big mistakes," I said, confused. "I really hurt a lot of people. Especially Sara and Cameron, who I was supposed to love the most."

"I'm not doubting that those are big mistakes, bro," he said with a smile. "I'm saying those are human mistakes to make. All I heard was the story of a man who got injured and became lost."

"Yeah, but I *hurt* people, Eric."

"And look at you," he said, "showed up to the gym, barely scaping a buck-fifty on the scale, smelling of alcohol—"

"I deserved it! All of it," I said, cutting in, trying hard not to yell. "You can't just act like a monster and not brush it off, Eric. I spent nine months at Gram's house, filling myself with reminders of what I'd become. You can't let yourself forget that. I can't."

"Nine months?"

"I can't make up for what I've done," I said, burying my head in my hands. With every breath, I became aware of my body. Frail. Brittle. Wrapped in paper-thin flesh.

"To who? To yourself or to Sara."

"I don't know."

"Listen, despite what you've done, the fact is, someone who is truly a monster wouldn't have felt the need to punish themselves," Eric said as we took a left onto a gravel road. "If you were truly the person you made yourself out to be, then why would you be here? Why would you punish yourself?"

I sat for a moment; my head filled with nothing but the sound of crunching gravel.

"Shame and guilt are not the emotions of the heartless. They come from good people who know they've gone against the foundations of their spirit. It's a sickness with only one cure."

"Yeah? What's that?" I said, looking over.

"Forgiveness of the self," he said as though the answer should have been obvious, "It's one thing to try and do better, but you got to do it from a place of self-love, or else you're building a foundation in the sand. How are you supposed to do better if you don't believe or deserve you can?"

"How am I supposed to know when I've forgiven myself? That I'm ready to move on? What does that even look like!?" *Was I ready to move on? Did I deserve to be someone better?*

"The fact that you're on this hike, in this gym, and going to school, I would say you've been ready for a while now, even if your conscious self wasn't ready to accept the truth," Eric said. "You want a moment of honesty?"

"Sure," I said, sitting back in my seat.

"I think you're scared to move on."

My heart stopped.

"I think you're scared because you've lived with the idea of being a bad guy for so long that you can't think of anything else to be," he said. "That or you're scared that you'll find out you really are the bad guy."

Game over. He had figured me out. "You're right. I am afraid that after all the hard work, I really am a piece of shit."

"Cody, I've known you for what, a month? I could tell from the moment we met that you weren't a bad guy. After

113

watching you in the gym, supporting others, being a part of our little community, it only confirmed it," he said, putting a hand on my shoulder. "You can't erase your mistakes, but you don't have to live there and punish yourself by dragging them around. I've known a lot of people who have done worse and never hurt themselves as much as you've done to yourself."

We pulled off onto the side of the road. Tall evergreen trees seemed to push in on the thin sliver of gravel, making the space in the car feel even smaller. The GPS chimed over the speakers, and then we melted back into the silence.

"It's time to move on," Eric said, unbuckling his seatbelt. "You have the warrior's spirit, but it yearns for a purpose far bigger than fighting the shadows of the past. Back when I was fighting my own shadows, I concluded my purpose was to teach people how to use fitness to achieve spiritual evolution. It became my next mission. You need to find your own."

I sat for a moment, nodding absently. I unbuckled, and we both got out of the SUV. The air was so clean that it almost hurt to breathe in. Surrounded by the immensity of grey mountain faces, I felt small, but there was more to it than that. I felt enchanted and numb as if a struggle was taking place in a distant part of me that I couldn't control. I fell into silence as I walked around to the front and leaned back on the hood. Eric walked around the other side and handed me my pack, which I had forgotten about.

"You can handle this, Cody. But I understand that it isn't easy to let go of the old way of thinking. Negative emotions have more staying power than the positive," he said, dropping his bag in the dirt. "If you need permission to move on, then this it. Your sentence is over. You're free to go."

"Free? Free to what?"

"Free to find your real purpose, brother. Time to discover the man you're meant to be," he said with a smile.

Hot tears on my face turned cold in the light breeze that rolled through the trees. I wiped them off on the inside of my shirt as I sank to the ground, pressing my head against the bumper. "How am I supposed to do that?"

"You'll figure it out. That's what heroes do. They figure it out, and they don't turn back." He reached down and offered me a hand. In the distance, we could hear the cars filled with the rest of the guys rumbling down the road, "Come on, the old life is over. What better way to celebrate than by climbing a mountain?"

I grabbed his forearm, and he pulled me up to my feet. "This is it, huh?"

"That's it," he said. "Let's go wait by the trailhead for the rest of the team."

"Yeah," I said, shouldering my pack, "let's do that."

Chapter Ten:
Summit

June 30th 2017, 12:04pm

Six of us had gathered at the base of Tumbledown. Some of the guys I recognized were from Optimal Self, like Ben, Eric, and Rob, the kettlebell instructor, but there were two other guys I had never seen before. I shook hands with the mystery gentlemen but forgot their names almost immediately; I didn't have the capacity for name retention at that moment. According to the aging map behind the fogged-up plexiglass, the summit was only 3,000ft, and some change from the base. Not a strenuous hike by any means, but it was the most challenging physical thing I had attempted since getting off my cane. As we began the long march up the mountain, I knew I should have been more intimidated at the prospect of a hike, knowing my body was going to feel trashed, but something was shifting at my core, detaching my mind from the dull throbbing in my hips.

The air was soft and full of summer, smelling of broken branches and soil. Brilliant shades of greens and greys of the forest only floated past me, unable to be rendered in my mind, crowded out from the conversation in the car. Which proved just as elusive to hold on to. The group had formed just ahead of me, with Eric at its center. They were talking and joking around as we pushed our way up the trails. Though they were only five or so feet ahead of me, I couldn't hear them, their voices drowned out by the slow and rhythmic breathing which filled my ears. My thoughts were in a constant state of coming together and breaking apart, free of my control. I felt like an observer, trapped behind glass in my own mind, in awe of the chemistry that was taking place.

"Hey man, you good?" came a baritone voice that jarred me back into reality. Rob was looking back at me, his bare shoulders already turning red from the straps on his backpack. "You want some trail mix or something?" he said, offering me a half-full bag.

"I'm good, man. I appreciate it, though," I said, looking around. The whole group had come to a quick stop for water, and I had absently kept walking.

"Alright," he said, slipping his bag off to one side. "I know you've only been at the gym for like a month, but you seem like a cool guy," he said, putting the bag of trail mix away.

I gave a small laugh. "Thanks, I try. I've meant to come to one of your kettlebell classes, but I never seem to find the time."

"That's okay. I'm sure Eric can teach you some stuff, but next time I'm in there, I'll give you like a mini-lesson, for sure."

"Yeah, awesome, I'd like that." I smiled.

"Dope," he said as the group began to take off again.

My thoughts drifted back to Eric's conversation, and I knew he was right about me being afraid. What would it mean if, at the bottom of it all, I wasn't built to have a family? It's not like I didn't know people who were like that. Even worse, what if I was a good person? How are you supposed to live with those mistakes and pretend like everything was alright? The sun flickered behind summer leaves, sparkling as if we were deep under the water. Thinking over the past two years filled me with so much hurt, I thought of all the ways I had tried to drown out the pain. Alcohol. Overdosing on Benadryl to sleep eighteen hours a day. Trying to kill myself. Why? Staring down at my shoes, I watched the ground move below me like a treadmill.

Would it have been easier to just not care? Yeah. But I was unable to divorce myself from my mistakes. If I can't shut off the shame, and can't run, then what? Punishment? I bit the inside of my cheek. I knew Sara wouldn't forgive me. I would always be the failed husband and father to her. I had earned her low opinion through years of pain and neglect. But what about me? I shivered in the heat of the day. My mind rolled back to the black nights spent living in Gram's attic. If I was honest, I didn't have the energy to punish myself anymore. The self-loathing had lost its sting, and reminding myself, I didn't deserve love felt more like a fact than an emotional flogging. When I showed up to Optimal Self and told Eric that I no longer wanted to live like this, my subconscious asked for something more challenging. Freedom. Not from pain, but the freedom to move on.

"Hey, bro, be careful coming up, okay? The iron rails are slippery!"

I found myself staring up into a vertical rock tunnel with a ladder of dark iron rungs.

"Alright!" I yelled up the rock chute, trying to hide my surprise.

"Wait until you get to the top!"

I began to climb into the twilight of the tunnel, which was so cold I swore I saw my breath, if only for a second. Eric held out his hand and pulled me up onto the trail.

"We are almost to the top. Your legs feeling alright?"

"Yeah, man," I said.

"How's your head?"

"You know, better than it's been in a long time."

"Good bro, glad to hear it."

"There is just a piece or two I need to put into place before I'm ready to move on," I said.

"You'll figure it out," he said, patting me on the back, "Codessious! Conqueror of many mountains! Or at least many hills!"

I gave a tired laugh as I joined the rest of the group. For the first time since the hike had begun, I felt as if I had come back to my body. I became aware that the sun was beating down on my neck and the acute pain in my hips.

"You've seriously never been here before?" Ben asked as we started walking.

"No, my parents didn't take us places like this," I said.

"That's a shame," he said, wiping sweaty hands on his shorts.

I shrugged. "It's fine if you don't know what you're missing out on, I guess."

Rounding the trailhead, I came face to face with the promised summit. Nestled in a shallow granite valley,

119

surrounded by a sentinel of trees, where the black waters of a small pond, reflecting back the thin wisps of clouds overhead. Making our way along the shore of worn granite slabs, I spotted a small island in the middle of the dark water. Smiling to myself, I was glad that I hadn't missed out on this trip. After Sara and Cameron had left the day before, it had taken all I had to get out of bed this morning.

"This is beautiful," I whispered to myself.

"We're over here, bro!" Eric yelled from further down the slab where the guys were sitting down.

"Sorry!"

Taking a seat on the granite, I took off my boots and socks to dry my feet. Using my backpack as a pillow, I stretched out and let the sun make me drowsy. The cool air nipped at my skin and ebbed and flowed to the sounds of the water. With my body shut down, my mind finally began to hum once again, though this time, absent was the heaviness that had followed me up the mountain. I didn't know what 'getting better' would look like, but up here, pressed against the clouds, it felt like it was time to let go. For years, I'd had a long and painful grasp on an image of myself as a wasted shell of a human life who only served to make people miserable. In this, I found my only semblance of identity, which gave me purpose and a mission to punish myself for all of those wrongdoings. My body withering away all the while. Acceptable collateral damage.

I couldn't remember what it was like to be present in my own skin until this moment on the granite shores of a mountain lake. My body and mind had become separate beings over the years, estranged from one another. If it hadn't been for that hangover a month back, there was a real chance that I'd still be oblivious to the fact that they both had become so run down. Underneath the sun, my joints ached with an unnamable new dimension that tethered my mind and body together in a way I can't remember experiencing. I felt present in the ache. For the first time, I existed all at once, and I breathed it in earnest.

"You going to get in the water?" Rob's voice cut in. Shielding my eyes, I could see he had traded in his hiking pants for board shorts that he must have packed away.

"Y'all actually going to go swimming in that water?" I asked, sitting up looking down at the dark ripples that shivered across the surface of the pond.

"After a hike like that? Oh, for sure," he said. "We all are."

Off to my left, I noticed the whole group was changing openly into swimming trunks, an item no one had told me to bring. I tossed the idea back and forth in my head, but I hesitated at the thought of being shirtless in front of a group of guys who were miles above my current aesthetic situation.

"I don't know, man, looks kinda cold," I said, trying to pass on the offer. "Plus, I don't have extra clothes."

"I'm sure someone has shorts they can hook you up with, plus it's not really that cold," he said. "The whole pond gets so much sunlight that it's practically a heated pool."

"Ah," I said, "Well, I guess I don—"

"CODY!" Eric yelled from higher up on the granite slab. "You getting in on this?"

"Yeah!"

"Cool, man, I'll go ask if anyone has any extra shorts for you."

"Thanks," I said, watching him leave and skip back up to where the rest of the group was hanging out.

Taking a deep breath, I stood up. My knees quivered as I undid the buckle of my pants and let them fall onto the rock in a crumpled ball. Though my legs resembled two hairy PVC pipes, it didn't bother me to be half-naked in the traditional sense. Six years in the Marine Corps, I had been naked in front of strangers more times than I could remember, but this was different. I was no longer that person. My mind kept flashing back to the pale and broken body in the mirror. Would they see what I saw?

"Here are some shorts," Rob said, tossing me a pair of red and white trim board shorts that looked a little too big in the waist.

With that, Rob waded into the water as the other guys joined him, talking in indistinct conversation. Watching them move around in the dark water, I felt like the awkward kid in high school.

"CODY, LET'S GO!" Eric said. The whole group was chest-deep in front of me with him at its center. "We're going to the island."

Unable to back out, I did my best to let go of the impossible task of predicting their judgment upon seeing my atrophied body. If I didn't look them in the eyes, maybe I wouldn't be able to feel them picking my flaws apart. Pulling the sweat-soaked shirt over my head, I could feel the heat of the afternoon sun brush across my bare skin. I felt naked. The guys began to break ranks and start making their way to the small island just a stone's throw from the shore, and I breathed a sigh of relief. Rob was right. The water was almost obscenely warm. With the mud pressing its way between my toes, it felt as if I was walking into the belly of some terrible monster.

"You're looking good, dude!" Ben said, his head bobbing in the water.

"Oh, uh, thanks," I said, my cheeks going red in the sun.

"I know it's only been a month, but your chest is looking a lot better," he said. "I don't mean to sound rude, but whenever you'd change into clean shirts, it was really easy to see your ribs, but now there is a little something there!"

"Heh." I didn't know how to feel about someone watching me when I was oblivious. But, on the other hand, it felt validating. "I'm glad someone else can see some kinda change," I said, looking down at my gleaming white torso.

"Usually, you're the last one to notice," he said. "That's just the way it is sometimes. I don't want to be weird or anything, but I find it really motivating when I get told about the progress I make, so maybe I'm just projecting."

"No, I actually appreciate it," I said, sinking deeper into the water. "I'm not sure how to take compliments honestly, just because I don't hear them a lot, so I always get sort of suspicious."

Ben furrowed his eyebrows in confusion. "Huh?"

"What I meant to say was, I'm not…great at being kind with myself. When I hear compliments, I think the person is just lying to me. Which I recognize is not great, and I am working on it."

"Okay, yeah, I can see that. Hey man, sometimes people just mean what they say, you know? And I meant it. I can see physical improvements on your body brought on by hard work."

I smiled. "Thanks, man."

With the water up to my chest, I knew I had waded in as far as I could go and that it was time to join the rest of the group on the island. With a sharp inhale, I kicked against the muddy bottom of the pond and threw myself into the black water, the world temporarily disappearing in a rush of noise.

Chapter Eleven:
The Black Bus

July 16th, 2017, 11:03am

"You mean to tell me you didn't see that giant bus parked in front of The Green Hand?" Courtney's blue eyes flashed in the glow of the coffee house lights. It was strange how much had happened since wandering off her porch what seemed like ages ago.

"I mean, The Green Hand is a super cool bookstore, but I haven't been there in a while," I said, with a defensive shrug.

"Cody Mower, I swear you are the most unobservant person I've ever met, now move out of the way. I have a customer," she said, waving me aside.

Since getting back from that trip with Eric a few weeks ago, I tried to make it a point to be around my friends more often. Though Speckled Axe was a pretty busy place, Courtney was kind enough to let me stick around longer than I should. Tucking myself into a stubby excuse for a hallway in front of the cash register, I sipped my cold brew and watched. A short brown-haired woman approached the counter with an expensive-looking purse and bug-eyed sunglasses. She spoke with a thick New York accent, which quickly escalated into an irritable bark as she began to argue with Courtney about some sort of exotic roast that Speckled didn't have.

"I'm sorry, sweetie, there is nothing I can do. Kopi luwak is just not something we have at the store," Courtney said with a smile.

Slouching her shoulders, the woman turned towards the door. "Well, I suppose it's not your fault, but I told my husband I didn't want to go to Maine for reasons like this."

"Okay, you have a good day now," Courtney said to her back.

I made my way back to the counter. "What the hell was that?" I asked once the woman had safely left the shop.

"God damn tourists is what *that* was," she said, shaking her head. "The rich ones from New York or New Jersey are always the worst."

"Why do you put up with it?" I said, putting my empty coffee down.

Turning to the fridge behind her, she took out a large jug of cold brew and refilled my glass. "Apart from needing to pay for rent, I put up with it because for every dozen assholes, I get to meet people like you."

"Surely you can meet better people," I said, shaking my head. "But I couldn't do what you do. Having to put on an act for ungrateful people? No, thank you."

"You put up with me, don't you?"

"That is not the same."

"You mean, you don't think I'm an asshole?" Courtney said, putting her hands on her hips, her face bent in a scowl.

"I think you're good at pretending to be," I said, rolling my eyes.

She blushed and dropped her hands back to her side. "Don't tell anyone, okay?"

"Sure."

"Good," she said, "but, anyway, there is a giant pitch-black bus outside The Green Hand. When I was walking by it, they had the stairs going up into it, and it looks like a whole other book shop. It looks spooky and right up your alley."

"Spooky, you say?"

"Absolutely terrifying," she said, leaning across the counter.

Chapter Twelve:
S&EM

July 16th, 2017, 11:34am

My legs had begun to sweat inside my jeans in the early afternoon sun as I made my way up the block from Speckled Ax to investigate this mysterious bus that had also been calling Congress Street home. Passing the entry door of my apartment building on my way to the bus, I stepped into the shade of its massive steel awning, trying to decide if I wanted to change into shorts but looking up the road, I changed my mind. Then, peeking over a crest of red brick sidewalk, the words BOOKMOBILE shimmered in the heat like a neon light, drawing me in.

The bus felt like an uneasy stranger in the vibrant city streets of Portland. Taking up two and a half parking spots in front of *The Green Hand*, it cut an intimidating figure with its large black body and hungry white fangs stenciled above the front wheels. The words *The Road Virus* had been hand-painted in large white letters next to the small emergency door on the side. I was so caught up on the bus that I hadn't noticed the man standing next to me.

"What do you think?" he said, making me jump. The man was about my height, with a faded neon yellow mohawk, which made him appear taller than he was. On his nose sat a pair of perfectly round sunglasses that obscured the whole top half of his face. Reaching into his shorts, he pulled out a crushed-up box of American Spirits and a zippo lighter.

"It's pretty badass."

Without a word, he flipped open his lighter and snapped it across his faded Fangoria tank-top for a spark and casually lit his cigarette. "Thanks," he said, blowing smoke off to the side.

"This is your bus?" I asked.

Taking another drag of his cigarette, he shrugged and pointed to the passenger side window. "Actually, she belongs to both my partner Em and me."

I saw a swipe of pink hair inside the bus sitting in the shadows and shoved my hands in my pockets. I became aware of the uneven breaths I was taking as I realized I had no idea what to do. "Where you guys from?" I asked, trying not to sound awkward.

"California," he said, flicking some ash onto the brick below, the sun catching the dangling chains of his silver earrings. "We both are. The Road Virus is sort of a dream of ours come to life."

"You're lucky to be able to live your dream like this. I'm happy for you," I said. Smiling, I could feel the gravity of my own life pressing down around me. For a moment, I felt a twinge of envy, but it quickly vanished as I knew I didn't possess a dream that could be considered concrete enough to go after.

"It was a lot of work. We sold everything to get here," he said, taking a final pull from his cigarette. "I mean seriously everything, that bus is the only thing we have now."

"That's fucking intense."

"Sometimes you got to be intense," he said, snuffing the butt out on his Doc Martins and putting it in his pocket. "What about you?"

The question took me by surprise, and I just started to ramble, "Me? I'm studying English at the university down the road. Just moved to Portland a few months ago. Trying to move on from some military and broken marriage stuff. I don't have a big goal yet, just trying to put my soul together if that makes sense."

The man chuckled. "It'll come to you, I'm sure. My name is S, by the way."

"Uh, I'm Cody," I said, puzzling over the short name.

"I see that look on your face," he said, moving towards the closed side door. "Yes, my name is 'S,' and yes, it is short for something else."

"Cody is short for Codessious if that makes you feel better," I said, looking at my feet.

"Is it?"

"No," I said, my cheeks getting hot in the sun with embarrassment. "It's just something my friends call me sometimes."

S looked as if he was about to say something but changed his mind. After a moment, he looked back at me. "We don't open for another two hours or so. Why don't you drop in then, and I'll show you the bus?"

"Yeah, sure."

S gave a small wave shutting the door behind with a metallic click, and I was left standing alone on the sidewalk.

Shuffling back down to my apartment, I kept staring at my shoes, running the conversation through my head, wondering if I had come off too strong with the whole "broken marriage and no goals" talk. *Definitely*, I thought, opening the door to the apartment building. There wasn't anything I could do about it now.

"Where've you been?" Casey asked as I shut the door behind me.

"I grabbed some coffee at Speckled, investigated a bookmobile," I said, taking a seat at the desk.

"You mean that giant black bus up the road?"

"Yeah, you've been there already?" I said, raising an eyebrow.

"Uh, no, but it has been there for like four days now," he said.

"Four days!? I thought it just got here!"

"Brother, it is a giant black bus. How. How do you not notice it? All you have to do is physically look down that side of the road when you cross the street into the gym. It takes up thirty percent of the street," he said, shaking his head.

Leaning back in the chair, I shrugged. "I've been thinking about a lot of things lately, I guess."

"Understandable. You seem a lot calmer since coming back from the mountains."

"I don't know if it's about being calm. Eric helped me realize some important shit about myself, but now… it's like, what do I do with it?"

"What do you mean?"

"For the first time in my life, I don't feel like a piece of shit. Which is good, but now what? Self-loathing used to be my trademark. What am I supposed to replace that with? What am I supposed to do with my life now that I don't hate myself?" I said, leaning over to his side of the desk.

"You know, most people find a job," Casey said, getting up and turning on the coffee pot.

"Can you be useful for like three seconds?" I groaned, throwing myself back into my seat.

"Bish," he said, taking a mug from the cupboard, "Don't put that on me. I'm not a life advice expert. Like, I'm here for you, and I'm happy you sorted some shit out, but you got to figure that part out on your own like the rest of us schmucks."

"No, that's…not what I mean."

"Then what is it?" he said, pushing his glasses up. The Kurieg sputtered hot coffee and steam behind him, filling the small room with the aroma of dark roast.

"It's just like, I feel like I'm brand new into the world. There is so much out there, and it's overwhelming."

"Is that so bad?"

"What do you mean?"

Taking his coffee and sitting back down at the desk, he looked at me. "What I mean is, while most people by this point are stuck in whatever job or whatever lifestyle, you're not. So, don't rush it. Figure it out."

"How, though?"

"Oh my god," Casey slapped his forehead. "Figure it out!"

"Some help," I said, rolling my eyes.

The truth was I didn't know what I wanted to do with my life because I never thought I was going to make it this far. Never could I have conceived a life that wasn't rooted in the idea of that shattered thing I had glimpsed in the mirror. Spinning in my seat, I still had an hour and a half before the bus opened, so I crawled into my bean bag in front of the window and closed my eyes. With my face in the sun, I took stock of the things I knew about myself in an attempt to divine some sort of direction to go in.

My names, Cody and I:

1. Read too many books.
2. Drink too much coffee.
3. Enjoy talking to people at Optimal Self.
4. Watch too much YouTube.

Turning to the other side, I accessed my mental list from behind my eyelids. It felt too superficial. *Come on, Cody, think of shit that matters.*

My name's Cody, and I:

1. I am learning to be okay.
2. Enjoy making friends.
3. Want to mean something to my community.
4. Don't want to make the same mistakes again that put me here.
5. Want to be the first brother to get a degree.
6. Want to be the kind of dad I never had.
7. Miss being Sara's husband.

I miss being a husband and father. I didn't know how to hold that phrase. It slipped around in my head in a swirl of emotions I couldn't articulate. Memories of a once happy marriage were bumping against the recent empty sex Sara

133

and I had in the bathroom made my stomach hurt. *It's just different now*. I could hear myself saying to her, again and again. Although at the time I couldn't explain why it had felt so different, thinking about it now, I knew what it was. It was sex without love. A moment of desperation made my insides churn. I don't want desperation in my life anymore. I don't want to feel like a stranger to her anymore. I shook my head, picturing her and Cameron back in the parking garage. If only the hike at Tumbledown had come sooner. Maybe I could have told her how I felt.

"You okay?" Casey said from his desk.

"Yeah," I said, slowly realizing how strange I looked, pressing at the side of my head like I was trying to keep it together.

"If people from the sidewalk looked up through the window, they might think you were crazy." He laughed.

"Who says I'm not?"

"You want to watch Markipler? He just uploaded a new *Try Not to Laugh* challenge."

"Yeah, sure," I said, getting up out of the window, leaving the thought behind me, "at least until the bus opens up."

Chapter Thirteen:
With Friends Like These

July 16th, 2017, 3:14pm

Stepping up into *The Road Virus*, the humid air melted away into a light mix of Pinesol and aging library musk, with a subtle hint of ash. The floor was made from planks of grey wood, which contrasted nicely with the long rows of black shelving. Though the space on the bus was small, it was jammed with hundreds of books, whose spines ranged from brand new to falling apart. Jutting out from the packed shelves were handmade signs which said things like *Queer Lit*, *Sci-fi*. *Body Horror*, *Cyberpunk*, and so on.

"Oh, hey, you made it," S said from the driver's seat behind a handmade wooden counter, "Feel free to look around." The font of the bus was filled with burned-out heads of baby dolls glued to the dash, and from the ceiling, bits of animal bones on strings dangled like windchimes. In the passenger seat, dressed all in black, was the woman who I assumed was Em. Her pink pixie cut a bold splash of color that rebelled against the dark.

"This is beautiful," was all I managed to say.

"Aw, thank you," Em said, peering over from the passenger seat. "Wait, are you the guy S was talking about?" She lifted a one-eyed chihuahua from her lap onto her shoulder as she spoke.

"Yeah, that's him," S said from behind his beard and dark glasses, "The guy with the Greek name."

With a pang of embarrassment, I relented, "I'm not funny. I get it, okay?"

"Don't worry about him," Em said, standing up and crossing the threshold into the bookstore. Putting a hand on my shoulder, she assured me. "It is S who has the horrible sense of humor, like right now."

"You're Em, right?" I asked.

"Emily, but yeah, Em, whatever works." The one-eyed dog was fast asleep on her shoulder. Moving from shelf to shelf, Emily began pushing and rearranging misplaced books.

"I'm Cody."

"Good to meet you, Cody," Emily said, shaking my hand. "Sorry, I can't stand it when the books get jumbled. It's a habit from when I used to be a school librarian. Let me tell you, elementary kids are atrocious when it comes to handling books, and this gets on my nerves."

My brain jolted, unable to place this goth lady with a pixie cut scanning in a worn copy of *Captain Underpants* back into the stacks. "That's fair enough," I said, still puzzled.

"Before I met S, I lived a completely different life in California. I was over-weight, submissive, married to your textbook alcoholic, abusive lawyer husband." Taking a seat back in the front of the bus, she put the dog into a small plastic crate between the two seats, "I have a master's degree in library sciences, which yes, is a real thing, and I worked at a private school for celebrity children who made my life almost as unbearable as the husband."

"Oh. I'm glad you're in a happier relationship now." The response felt inadequate and clunky. *I need to work on small talk*, I noted.

"Thanks, me too," she said, smiling again. "But what about you? Are you looking for anything particular?"

"That's a hard question," I said, leaning against one of the bookshelves, "I've only recently discovered that I'm not walking a black hole that consumes the life force of everyone I come in contact with. I'm trying to learn to be okay with that. So, I don't think I know what I'm looking for."

Emily nodded slowly. "I was talking about looking for something to read, but I think I want to hear more of this story."

I bit the inside of my cheek. "Ah. I'm an idiot, sorry."

S cut in, "Don't be sorry. Em's got secret powers like that. She always gets people to talk. You should hear some of the stories that come through the bus. It can get pretty intense."

My brain went back and forth for a minute on what to do next. It was one thing to tell Eric my story, but the idea of telling it to total strangers had never crossed my mind. Yet, the idea of telling it again didn't feel like a boundary.

"You don't have to say anything," Emily said.

"You know," I said, "I've held on to so much pain for so long that having an opportunity to speak it out loud…is an opportunity to remind myself not to go back."

"I like that," S said. "You don't want to forget where you came from."

For the next 45 minutes, I told both of them my story as honestly as possible, only pausing whenever a customer had entered to browse the shelves. I covered everything from my failed marriage, my brain injury, and the horrible hangover that led me to Optimal Self. When I finished, Emily got out of her seat and threw her arms around me, holding me gently. This took me by surprise, and for a moment, I was filled with an overwhelming sense of fear that made me want to run. But that fear dissolved in her arms, and I put my arms around her and hugged her back.

"I'm so proud of you," she said at last.

"Thank you."

Letting me go, I looked over at S, who was chewing on the end of a pen. "That's one hell of a story, man. I'm glad you're here."

"I'm sorry for taking so long about myself. But I appreciate you both for sitting through it," I said.

"Hunny, I asked to hear your story!" Emily said, "Don't apologize for something I asked for."

"What about you two? How did you end up with a bookmobile of all things?

Emily pointed at herself, "Hello, yes, librarian here. I like books."

S laughed. "And I'm the queer, horror lover. Put those both together, and you get the bookmobile."

"Yes, but to give up everything back in California to just roam the US takes some serious stones."

"As I'm sure you're aware, life is short and unpredictable. Both S and I knew each other from a writing group in San Francisco, and we were both pretty unhappy. He had his demons, and I had mine. We got to know each other pretty well over a few months. After that, we decided to give it all up for the bookmobile."

"Pretty radical thing to do."

"Yeah, fuck it, why not? What is the alternative? Suffer silently or keep dreaming about one day getting off up your ass, tell the boss to shove it, and live the life you want? Nah, I don't think either of us wanted to live that life. You're only on this planet for a set number of years, and I know I don't want to die unfulfilled," Emily said, running her hands along the counter.

"Even if this whole thing crashes and burns, it's worth it. We've already been on the road for two months and have so many crazy stories," S said.

Listening to them filled me with a sense of optimism for my own unknown future.

"Is there something you've always wanted to do?" Emily said.

I shrugged. "I don't know. Like I said, I'm still trying to figure that out."

We fell back into talking about life. S told me stories of his punk years on the streets of San Francisco, stealing food, doing drugs, and living the real anarchist dream. It was such a dark and wild story that it seemed more fiction than fact, but the pain in his voice and scars on his body, which he showed off, told me that it was the truth. Marveling at his life, it stood in stark contrast to Emily's upper-class New England upbringing and wealthy suburban existence in the city. But then again, life brings people together in strange ways. After all, here we were. Three broken people comparing scars and swapping stories as the summer evening shadows grew long across the city street.

Checking my watch at a glance, it was sometime past 11pm, and I realized how hungry I'd become. "Well, guys, I'm going to head on home. My brother is probably worried about me."

"Alright, sweetie," Emily said, getting out of her seat to give me a parting hug, "don't be afraid to come back tomorrow and hang out with us!"

"Really? You want to see me again?"

"Oh yes, I think she likes you," S said.

"I love him!" Emily declared. "He fits right in on our little bus of misfits."

I smiled.

"Looks like you're coming back tomorrow then?" S said, standing up giving me a hug.

"Yeah, for sure. This has been such a strange and fantastic night, and I want more," I said. "Also, if you need any help on the bus, let me know. I don't want to get paid or anything. I just really like you guys."

"Of course, sweetie."

When I opened the apartment door, Casey was sitting at this desk watching YouTube in the dark. Switching the light on, he jumped.

"Oh my God!" he said, spinning around in his chair.

"You alright?"

"Fuck, you scared me."

"Sorry, man."

"How was the bookmobile? Were you there the whole time, or did you go out?"

"No, dude, I was there the whole time. And I think I made friends?"

Casey's raised both eyebrows, "You made friends, huh?"

"Yeah. I really did."

Chapter Fourteen:
Whisked Away

July 21ˢᵗ, 2017 2:36pm

Over the next couple of days, I went to visit S or Sade and Emily in between school and the gym. I was still sweating from the afternoon deadlift session as I knocked on the bus door. Officially *The Road Virus* wouldn't be open for another five hours, but they made an exception for me. I could see Emily wave to me from the window of the passenger seat, and I held my breath as Sade unlocked the door and let me in. I shivered as I stepped up into the darkened stacks of books. Somewhere in the corner, a shadow moved, and I frowned. Luci or LuciPurr, if you wanted to use her full name, was a large black cat who hated people. She was Sade's cat, which was about the extent of the people she let near her. When the store was open, she would shove herself into some corner and quietly hiss away.

"Hey, guys, what's up?" I said, taking my usual seat on the floor next to the checkout counter. Something was off. A tension swirled around the bus, and I tried to ignore it, but Em cut straight to the chase.

"Listen, babe, there isn't an easy way to say this, so I'm just going to let it out. We've been in Portland a lot longer than we planned on. But, if we're both being honest, a large part of it is because of you. Portland has been so amazing to us, but the thing about traveling bookmobiles is that...well, they travel."

"We're taking Jolene up north to make the obligatory trip up to Stephen King's place, but then we're out of New England," Sade said, taking off his round sunglasses.

My heart sank. I hadn't known Sade and Em for years or anything, but they were the rare sort of people that you didn't need to know your whole life to feel attached to them. "When do you guys leave?"

"Friday, we are going to head up, open shop in Bangor for a few days, and be out of the state by August. Honestly, we're trying to make it to Cali for Wasteland Weekend," Sade said.

Getting out of her seat, Emily kneeled next to me on the floor. Brushing her pink hair out of the way she smiled. "Cody, you'd love it. It's like a whole weekend where everyone pretends that you're living in a post-apocalyptic hell. You should really come see it."

I gave a pitiful shrug. The reality was beginning to set in that I was about to lose friends I had just made. Kicking myself mentally, I figured that's what I get for investing so much time into people whose very job was to travel. Rookie mistake.

"No, we mean it," Sade leaning on the table looking down at me. "We'd like you to come see it. With us."

"I can't afford a plane ticket to California, guys."

"Who said anything about flying?"

"Hun, what Sade and I are saying is that we'd like you to come travel with us here on Jolene. We've heard enough of your story and been around you long enough to know it would feel right having you here," Em said, putting her hand on my shoulder.

"Plus, haven't you ever just wanted to run away and start over? Join the circus! But you know, instead of a circus, it's a bus full of books." Sade laughed.

The gears in my head screeched to a halt as I tried to process what was going on. Was this even real life? I felt like I had been handed a golden ticket to the biggest mystery prize there ever was. My stomach began to tighten, but as I sat on the floor. I couldn't find a strong enough reason to say no, but yes didn't fall out of my mouth either. This seemed like one of those decisions when you said yes. It was because every fiber of your body was screaming YES.

Sensing my struggle, Emily broke in once again, "You don't have to. There is absolutely no pressure, but we think this could be as healing for you as it was for us."

"Would it be possible to do a test run? Come with y'all to Bangor and then make a decision after?" I chose my words carefully. Maybe Emily was right. Maybe this was the next step on my journey? After healing on the mountain top, I was supposed to travel the world on a bus full of horror books.

"That's not a bad idea. If that's what you need, hun, then we are here for it!"

"Once you get a taste for bus life, I don't think you'll go back. The freedom is outrageous," Sade said, stretching in his seat.

"Things you should bring, your own toothbrush obviously, a few changes of clothes, a pillow for sure—"

"Em, I was a professional camper for six years in the military. So, I know what to bring for a field op."

"Right, of course, sorry! I slipped into a mothering mode rather quickly there, didn't I?"

"It's okay."

"I'm so excited! SADE, HE'S GONNA BE WITH US ON THE BUS!"

"I know, I was here when he said it" Sade said, shaking his head.

The rest of the night, Emily was in a good mood. I hung around like I had been the other nights, helping to sell books and talk to customers, but a strange feeling was dampening my mood. I wasn't nervous about Sade or Em selling my organs on the black market or anything like that, but I did wonder, what if I enjoyed being on the road? Would it be that easy to leave school and Casey behind? What about Cameron and Sara? So many questions began to spring up, and my brain had no answer and nowhere to put them, so I shoved it as far back as I could because, at the end of the day, there was only one way to figure any of this out. I had to go.

We finished dinner a little after ten, and Emily told me to go home and get some rest. Opening the door of the apartment, I found that Casey was still where he always seemed to be at his desk, hunched over his laptop in the dark. Kicking off my shoes, I took a seat across from him and booted up my laptop.

"How was it?"

"The bookmobile was good, like always," I said, looking over the books that dived out halves of the desk.

"You still up for watching some Markipler?"

145

"I'm going with them for a week."

"Huh?" Casey said, taking off his headphones.

"The bookmobile. They're headed up north for a week, and I'm going to go with them." I sounded like I was trying to convince myself that this was a reality.

"What about school? And like…the gym? I thought you loved that shit."

"I do. I don't know, man, haven't you ever wanted to like join the circus or something?"

"The circus? Uh, can't say that I have."

"Listen, it's just for a week. Who knows, but it's not an opportunity that just happens to fall in your lap every day. A part of me thinks it would be a stupid thing to turn down."

Casey paused for a moment and shrugged. "You're an adult. I haven't really thought about it, but I'd take a chance if I were in your shoes. Just don't get murdered."

I decided not to tell him how far out the offer extended.

Chapter Fifteen:
Cold Brews and
American Spirits

July 26th, 2017. 8:12am

"Good luck," Casey said, turning around at his desk. His voice was flat. I knew he was annoyed that I was going to be gone for a bit.

I was half out of the door with my backpack full of clothes and a bulky beanbag under my arm. "You could help, you know."

"I don't want to stand in the way of your independence."

"My ass."

"Listen, if you get used to me helping you now, you're going to struggle even harder if I'm not there to help you on the way back."

"Whatever, you lanky gremlin," I said, the door closing behind me.

Halfway down the hall, I made the decision to take the stairs so I could throw my beanbag down the narrow hole that dropped all the way to the ground floor to save myself some time. Collecting my shit off the concrete, I was relieved to see Sade was standing on the other side of the glass door, the bus squeezed across four parking spaces behind him.

"Yo!" he said, helping me with the beanbag. "You ready to get this show on the road?"

"Yeah," I said, following up into the bus. I had never seen the bus in travel mode before. The books had been taken off the shelves, packed away in neat plastic totes that were bungeed to little hooks drilled into the floor.

"Did you say your goodbyes?"

"Goodbyes?"

Sade laughed. "I'm telling you once you get a taste for this life, I don't think you're going to want to back." He dropped my beanbag on the floor and walked to the front of the bus and began adjusting the side mirror.

"Hey, Chickadee!" Emily said, from behind the curtain that separated the retail space from their living area.

"Hey, Em!" I dropped my backpack into a corner, kicking it out of the way as Emily walked out, giving me a tight hug. She had spiked her pink hair into a mohawk, making her look like a badass Mad Max extra.

"I'm so excited you're coming with us!"

"Yeah, I thought it would be dumb not to try something new, you know?"

"Of course! What is life if not an adventure?" she said, taking her seat at the front of the bus.

"You're probably going to have to use your beanbag as a seat, which means seatbelt for you, I guess." He gave a deep laugh and turned the engine over.

I slid my beanbag between the gap in the counter, taking my seat. Staring out of the windshield, a wave of adrenaline washed its way through my body, making me feel queasy.

I'm actually doing this, I thought. *This is fucking insane.* I swallowed the urge to call the whole thing off as Sade pulled the bus out into the street. *It's too late now*, I told myself.

The radio on the bus didn't work, and after forty minutes on the road, the drone of the highway was starting to get old. Sade and Em never had the original hardware to the bus updated, so it lacked an MP3 jack or a CD player. But luckily, it had a built-in cassette player. As the guest of honor, I had the privilege to rummage through Sade's box of tapes picking out the music for the ride up north. It was an unorganized mess of plastic covers, some with torn and dirty paper artwork like Radio Head's *Pablo Honey* or The Eagles *Greatest Hits 1971-1975*. He also had some handwritten mixtapes, and I grabbed one that read *My Chemical Romance and Other Sad Shit*.

"What about this one?" I said, holding the tape up.

Emily took it and gave a tiny swoon. "A boy after my own heart! You know Sade made this for me when we started dating?"

"Pop that bitch in," Sade said, glancing over at Em. Cranking the radio up, the opening piano to *Black Parade* filled the bus. I could feel the tension build towards the song's opening line as we looked around at each other, taking a deep breath getting ready for Gerard to lead us.

"WHEN I WAS…A YOUNG BOY! MY FATHER! TOOK ME INTO THE CITY…TO SEE A MARCHING BAND!" We all screamed in unison, trying to hold back from laughing as we sang along. The farther we got into the mixtape, the more I had forgotten about the nervous feeling in my gut. I stopped wondering if I had made the wrong decision. Sitting there, screaming along to lyrics I still remember from high school, I felt my phone vibrating in my pocket. When I saw it was Sara, I felt like I had been yanked back down to earth. I hadn't told her where I was going. Did I even need to? I began feeling nauseous, watching her picture on my screen. Not knowing what to do I simply chose to ignore the call.

"You alright, sweet pea?" Emily said, shouting over the music.

"Yeah," I said, shaking my head, staring at my phone.

She looked unconvinced. "Did something happen? Is your brother, okay? We can bring you back if you need to."

"No, no, it's nothing. Casey's fine. I just had a stupid thought about school."

"Uh…huh."

"Everything is okay!" I said, putting my phone in my pocket.

"I won't pry, but if you want to talk, we are literally right here. You know us. We won't judge."

"I know."

"We are going to pull over soon for a smoke break, sweetie, okay? The GPS says there is a Dunkin at the truck stop. Maybe some coffee will help."

For the next twenty minutes, I laid back in my seat. My sudden change of mood had brought down the energy in the bus, and now no one was singing. It made me angry that I killed the atmosphere on the bus, which quickly turned into guilt. *Why does it matter if Sara knows I'm on the bus?* I thought. *I'm my own person now.* I felt like I was reasoning myself in circles for so long I didn't notice that the bus had pulled off the highway.

"You need a hand?" Sade asked, offering me his.

"Thanks," I said, as he pulled me out of my beanbag.

"Right, so I'm going to smoke."

I stepped out and wandered around the parking lot. Obviously, we couldn't go through the drive thru for coffee so why Sade took another drag off his American Spirit, Em and I walked nonchalantly into the Dunkin half of the gas station, trying to avoid eye contact with all of the gawking trucker drivers and out of staters on vacation, taken aback by the giant black bus we rode in on.

"You'll get used to it," Em said, squeezing my shoulder.

"It's fine. I used to think people were staring at me all the time, even when they weren't. Now that they are, I feel prepared for it somehow."

We stood in line, and I found myself thinking of Sara and Cameron. I was so lost in thought; I didn't see that Em had ordered for me. A large cold brew. Black, no cream, no sugar. I told her thank you and we walked back outside into the summer afternoon. There was a small metal picnic table off the side and my feet followed Emily once again until we were both sitting in silence under the sun.

"Was it Sara?"

"Huh?" Her guess caught me off-guard, and my silence let her in on the secret.

"She doesn't know you're on the bus, does she?"

"No."

"Why does it bother you?

"I'm not sure I can explain it. I know we have been split up for over a year, but even still I can't help but feel in the back of mind that everything I'm doing is wrong. Or maybe wrong isn't the right word. I just feel like something is off."

"I remember you saying you guys had been together for eight years, before you separated. That is a long time. Plus, you have a kid together so I can only imagine that after a while that sense of responsibility gets ingrained into you somehow," she said, looking at me.

"I mean, I think it's like the idea that if I really like the bus, then I'm going to be gone, gone. I'm not sure what do with that. What if we end up somewhere far away and I can't see Cameron? I don't know. How would I even explain that to anyone? Do I just quit school?"

Emily reached over and placed her hand over mine, "You know those are great questions to ask and I'm glad you're taking our offer so seriously, but sweetheart, this isn't something you need to have answers to right away. I would suggest though, you spend time thinking about why the thing with Sara bothers you so much?"

I gave a shrug and wrapped my hands around the slowly melting coffee which I still hadn't touched.

"Do you still love Sara?"

"I mean...we have a kid together." My palms began to sweat, and I couldn't tell if it was from the heat or something else.

"That's not what I meant. I mean, do you still see yourself getting back together with her?"

My thoughts flashed into a kaleidoscope of memories. A swirling mix of bitter and sweet that knotted up in my head. My stomach dropped as I thought about that night on the bathroom floor, and how I told her everything felt different. That was still true, but did different have to mean bad? I wasn't sure. I pulled my knees to my chest on the end of the table and finally sipped my coffee unsure of what to say back to her.

"Just take your time. Don't rush, the answers will come to you and the bus will always be here. Even if you get back home and change your mind, Sade and I will drive back and come get you, okay?"

"Okay," I said. "I'm sorry for killing the vibe in the bus earlier with my moping. I mean, yeah it was Sara who called, not Casey. I just didn't know what to do."

"Babe, it's alright. You have nothing to feel upset about. You've got a lot going on and we are here to help in any way we can."

"Thank you for being so kind to me."

"Are you kidding? Thank you for sharing so much of yourself with us. I can't tell you how healing it is to share stories with someone who has been through similar things. You fit in so well and we appreciate you."

We drank our coffees and watched as Sade flicked his cigarette out onto the asphalt and walked over to our little picnic party. "You guys almost ready? There is no rush or anything, but I'd like turn in early and we still have to find a place to shower."

"I thought that couple with the cute dog was letting us stay at their place?" Emily said.

"Kristy sent me a text and said they had some emergency family business. They said we could still use their house, but I don't know. Not feeling too comfy with just squatting in a house like that. What if the neighbors call the cops about the black bus outside? Rather not risk it."

"So, what now?"

I sat quietly, listening to Sade and Em as they listed off potential places to shower and park for the night. I felt like a child waiting for mom and dad to figure out where too next on a road trip. We had to go to Walmart to get cleaning supplies and Sade had suggested that we could shower in the bathrooms there, but Em dismissed the idea. After ten minutes of fruitless lists, Sade decided that we would just figure it out on the fly. We loaded back on the bus, and I nestled into my beanbag as Jolene's wheels squeaked out onto the highway.

"Hey Cody, I had this idea kicking around in my head if you're interested," Sade said, looking up into the mirror.

"Oh?"

"You're a writer. So, I was thinking, what if we did a blog post for publicity? You can just write about life out on the road and whatever, I think it would be really fun."

My eyes lit up. "For real!?"

"Yeah! You can do it in whatever style you want. But think of it as a road diary. You can use the laptop and I'll upload it."

"Thank you so much for offering! I would love to. Seriously."

"Awesome, I think it's going to be really cool. I even have an idea for the name."

"Let's hear it, babe," Em said cutting in from the passenger seat.

"What if we call it, *Eventually Everything*," he said, waving his hand like he was unveiling an attraction at a fair.

I nodded. "I like it. I like it a lot."

Chapter Sixteen:
Liminal

July 26th, 2017. 1:36pm

Despite growing up in Maine for most of my life, I had never been as far north as Bangor. My family was content with sticking to the same hills it called home since 1726. In fact, I had never even been to Portland until I had signed up for Marine Corps and took the oath of enlistment in the MEPS building. Bangor had its own reputation though, both for its crime and its ghost stories. It was the home of Stephen King after all. It was the third largest city in the state, it felt more like a tiny oasis lost in a sea of trees.

By the time *The Road Virus* had pulled into town, the sky was already turning a lead grey. When finally stopped and I took in the city for the first time, I wasn't quite sure what do it with it. Old brick buildings were crammed next to each other, painted various colors. Despite being a younger town than Portland, Bangor practically oozed melancholy from every empty window and stone doorway. There was very little foot traffic in town, so it gave it an eerie feeling of emptiness like you were walking around an abandoned movie set.

I wasn't the only one who was picking up on the feeling.

"Jesus Christ, I can tell why King calls this place home," Em said, looking up and down the sidewalk, not knowing which way to go.

Sade pointed to a large banner that was stretched across the road below. It read:

Summer Music in The Square All Week! July 24th Thru 30th

Emily frowned, "I don't know babe. Maybe we missed the big crowd when it started? Or do you want to wait for the weekend? It looks dead until the weekend. I'm not sure what we would even do in the meantime, because I doubt this it's worth opening up for until then."

"Sightsee?"

"Do you really think it's going to be worth it? This place reminds me of the *Walking Dead*."

"We can always play it by ear if you want. I'm not married to the idea of staying, but if the crowd is big enough, it would be helpful to get cash for the drive back down south."

"What do you think chickadee?" Em said, poking my arm.

"Umm," I hated being put on the spot and I really wasn't sure what answer I should give. "Let's stay. Who knows, it could be fun."

"Okay, it's decided then! Maybe we'll get lucky and see a ghost while we're out," she said, booping my nose before grabbing Sade's arm.

We walked aimlessly trying to get a feeling for the place we would be calling home for the next few days. The air smelled like wet concrete, absence of the mixing smells of restaurants and gasoline that one would expect in the city. There were signs for shops all up and down the streets, but the doors were all closed. A few times I thought about going into a place, but as soon as I would get to the closed door, I felt like an internal magnet was repelling me away and I would walk back to Sade and Em with a defeated look on my face.

"Can we head back to the bus?" I said after a while.

"Yeah. I'm ready for a nap," Sade said giving a stretch.

"Maybe tomorrow will be better?"

A heavy mist began to creep its way from between buildings and cracks in the sidewalk as we made our way back to the bus, shrouding the world in a deep silence.

Chapter Seventeen:
Rain

July 28th, 2017. 9:28am

I had been awake for a few hours by the time the other two had gotten up. There was a heavy rain outside which had woken me up, falling so hard that it sounded like hundreds of little frozen peas being dumped into an empty pot. Laying in the dark, I checked my phone and saw that I had missed two other calls from Sara, but she left no messages, voice mail or otherwise. Something had been stirring in me since Sara had left. Before the sex had happened, there was a moment where we had felt like a couple again. She felt like my friend. My wife. I think what was eating me up is that a part of me wanted that again, from her. Is that where the guilt about being on the bus was coming from?

I closed my eyes and listened to the rain. As much as I wanted to lean into the idea that we could be a couple I couldn't be sure if that is what *she* wanted. Or trust that these thoughts that I was having were even my own genuine thoughts or just echoes of something nostalgic and dead. Either way, I was too tired to pick apart these thoughts, so I just laid quietly in the dark and watched as the hazy light snuck into the bus through the large windshield. The rain never let up.

Around eight in the morning, Em slowly stirred and got dressed from behind the curtain that separated us.

"Good morning, chickadee," she whispered as Sade snored gently.

"Good morning," I whispered back.

She tiptoed to the front of the bus and sat in her seat. Cranking open the window, a sharp breezed whipped its way around the dark and she hastily lit a cigarette and blew the smoke out into the rain. Normally smoking inside the bus was against the rules, but it was too cold and wet to be outside.

"You want one?"

"No thank you," I said, taking a seat next to her. "Now if you had coffee stashed away somewhere, that would be great."

Em smiled and flicked some ash out of the window. "Maybe when Sade gets up, we'll drive to Tim Hortons or something, does that sound good?"

I nodded in the early morning light. "That sounds amazing."

"Great. Does grabbing some donuts sound good too?"

"Oh, fuck yes."

We sat in silence for a little bit longer before I turned my head and released a little bit of the thoughts that was stirring in my head. "You know what you had said to me early about wanting to be with Sara?"

Emily sat up and flicked the half-burnt cigarette out the window, "Yeah?"

159

I pressed my hands together in my lap and took a deep breath. "I think a part of me wants to be with her. Sincerely. But what if she doesn't accept me for the person I am now? My heart tells me that we could make this work, but I don't want to live with my past held over my head. Hell, I also don't know if these feelings are even my real feelings or if they're just dust kicked up from when she came to visit. I want to know, but how can I even be sure about anything?"

Taking a deep breath, Em sat still for a moment in her chair. "I wish I had the answers for you. I wish someone had the answers for me when I was going through my divorce. Although, for me whenever I started missing him, what I was really missing was this idealized version of him mixed with just wanting to have intimacy with someone."

"I've thought about having relationships with other people since her and I have been, but even the idea of it doesn't feel right. Not in the I feel like I'm cheating kind of way, but it fucks me up thinking I could share that kind of love with someone else."

"Well, at least we can cross that question off your list."

"What do you mean?"

"Hunny, I think your feelings for Sara, while complicated, are real. I knew that my feelings for my ex-husband were as shallow as you could be after we split. It was really easy to talk myself out of wanting to go back to him."

I turned my head out of the window. "I still love her." Hearing myself say the words out loud made my head dizzy. It felt like a confession. Like a dark secret. Even still all it did was edge me towards another rabbit hole I wasn't sure I was ready to fall down.

"Yes, you do."

"Now what?"

Em laughed. "I don't know. That's up to you. Call her maybe? Tell her how you feel? Or don't, go to school, stay on the bus with us. No matter what your choice is, don't make it something you're going to regret."

"I have to call her back today anyway. I missed two calls yesterday. But maybe breakfast first?"

"Of course, babe."

I had been so in my own head, I hardly remembered eating. My thoughts were a daze of memories and possibilities that played on loops, blocking out the rest of the morning. I knew we could be happy if we tried. If I tried. One of the biggest things that was holding me back was the past. It felt like an anvil dangling over my head, waiting to drop at a moment's notice. Even though I had given Sara reasons to mistrust me, to hate me, I didn't want to enter back into a relationship where the past could be used like a weapon during the first fight. I had lived with the shame and the guilt for so long, I just wasn't interested in being reminded of my mistakes as long as I lived. The last few years together of our marriage I learned that we could both be cruel, and I feared that some of that was still waiting for me, ready to undo all the work I had done on myself. I wanted to ask her, I needed to know if that was something she could get over? Did she honestly believe in a fresh start? In us?

The rest of the day was a kaleidoscope of slow-moving bodies in the town square, the rain keeping the crowds away. On a covered stage, local artists sang and strummed guitars to no one in the large coble stone square. Emily who

161

normally kept a relatively clean-cut appearance during business hours, smoked openly in the front seat. Even though no one said anything, we were all annoyed that this had been a waste of time. After three hours of a vacant bus, Sade tapped me on the shoulder asking me to help close shop. The rain had slowed into a mist, but it had gotten cold.

"I think I'm going to call her," I said, hosting the large wooden coffin we used as a display back into the bus.

"Yeah? Do you want us around for that?"

"No, I think I got it. I'm just going to go around back if that's okay?"

". We'll be inside when you're finished."

Shutting the door behind him, I was left alone in the quite empty of the square. By the time I put the phone to my ear, my heart and head were exhausted with all of the worries and fantasies that I didn't feel nervous or anxious. I just wanted to know.

"Hello?"

"Hey, it's me."

"I know. Why didn't you pick up?" Her voice was cold.

"I'm sort of busy with work, sorry."

"You got a job?"

"Sort of, not exactly. I'm working on a bookmobile with some friends."

"In Portland?"

"No, it's a bookmobile, so we travel," I said, shivering in the rain.

"What do you mean you work on a traveling bookmobile? Is this like a thing you're doing now?"

"Wha…? No. I don't know, look that's not why I'm calling."

Her voice went from cold to irritated.

"What do you mean you don't know? Who are these people?"

"They're my friends, I met them in Portland. Sade and Em are really nice. They have this horror themed bookmobile and they here from California. They travel the US selling books."

"Okay… are you planning to stay on with them or something?"

"I don't know, maybe for a while? It would be fun to road trip around and see the states. Honestly, haven't thought about it."

"So let me get this straight. You haven't picked up your phone because you're on some horror themed bookmobile with some people you've just met, who you may or may not be travelling the state with. Even though you are in school and have a son who wouldn't be able to see you because you'd be all over the place?"

She had backed me into a corner and this wasn't the conversation I planned on having. My thoughts and my mouth locked up as I struggled to think of what to say.

"Wow, Cody. Really responsible. Good Priorities! Anyway, your son wanted to talk to you. I'll just tell him you're too busy on a bookmobile or whatever you're doing now."

"What? I'm still in Maine!"

"Sure."

"Why are you being such a bitch about this? I'm not—"

"Don't call me a bitch."

"Can you just listen to me for like two seconds, Sara?"

"No. How about you—"

"Will you just shut up?! Fuck, I'm trying—" The line went dead, and the world faded back into existence. Defeated, I threw my hood on and began pacing in tight circles around the square as the mist turned once more into a drizzle. Even when I was trying to tell her I missed her, I was still getting shut down. *Why the fuck do I bother?* I found myself behind the shitty stage, punching at its frail aluminum walls, the white paint sticking to my reddening knuckles. Old feelings came flooding back into my body through still images of all those nights on the couch, arguments frozen at their peak, tears. So many tears.

Focusing on the pain in my hands in my chest, I had forgotten the most basic, life-saving rule that the Marine Corps had spent so long drilling into our heads. Situational awareness. In my fit, I had completely lost sight of the world around me and of the two men who were quickly closing in behind me. By the time I heard the heavy steps of their boots on the wet cobblestone, it was already too late to get away.

Chapter Eighteen:
The Haul

July 28th, 2017. 5:28pm

"Hey there, brother."

The gruff voice tore me from my feelings, and as I spun around, I was confronted by two lanky men. The taller one was clad in a white wife beater that had been soaked see-through in the rain. He had it tucked into a pair of dirty blue jeans so that you could see an obscenely large Bowie knife hanging off his belt. His arms were covered in a smattering of tattoos that looked like they had been collected in the basement of a friend of a friend. The second guy was much smaller, carrying a faded brown backpack and wearing an oversized black hoodie speckled with dandruff from his wiry beard. They stood on either side of me, unblinking against the rain. I could fear the fear move from my throat and back into my fists as my brain rapidly spun into flight or fight mode. Fight.

"Yeah?" I answered back, matching the taller guy's rough voice, my fists still curled.

"I got something you can take that anger out on," he said, wiping his wet hands on his dirty jeans. The guy in the black hoodie nodded beside him.

"Yeah, what's that?"

The tall guy looked behind him as if he was half expecting someone to be there before turning back to me, "A piece of pussy."

My fists dropped. "Huh?"

"I'm not a pimp or nothin'. I just have a friend that could use some money, is all," he said, almost embarrassed.

"Nah, man, I'm good."

The two men looked at each other, confused for a minute, before turning back to me. This time, the smaller guy opened his mouth, "Well, we saw from across the square that you looked pretty upset, man. So, we were just making sure you were alright. If you don't want sex, we got weed or something harder if you want."

I shrugged, not knowing what to do. I wanted to laugh at the Jay and Silent Bob not-pimps-nice drug dealer situation that was going on. Though what kept me from laughing was the fact the tall guy had a knife on his hip, and I only had my hands. "I'll take a cigarette if you got one."

The tall guy motioned to go around to the front of the stage to get out of the rain as we walked, he said, "I'm Cliff, and the smaller guy is Dale. We are just kind of stuck up here for a bit." Reaching into the bag, he pulled out a hard plastic case with a few packs of Marlboro Reds. "Hope reds are okay?"

"That's good, yeah."

We took our places around the empty stage, looking like a band playing music that no one wanted to hear. Cliff

166

passed around the lighter, and we each took turns exhaling a long stream of smoke. I wondered if Sade and Em would look out from the small side window of the bus and just be utterly confused at what was happening as I was.

"Well, I won't ask what your fight was about, but we all have bad days from time to time," Cliff said, leaning against the wall. Dale nodded in agreement.

"Tell me about it," I said, "I've been separated from my wife for a while. Bad shit happened in the military, I want to make up for it. I don't want her to hold it over my head the rest of my life. That's why I called her, and we ended up fighting about something else, so I didn't get to talk about it."

Dale chuckled, and Cliff looked at him. "Sounds familiar, eh bud?"

"Eight years in the army and two wives later," Dale said, speaking for the first time. His voice warbled as he talked, a stark difference from his tattooed partner.

"What's your name, by the way?" Cliff said, exhaling smoke.

"Austin," I said, not willing to give them any real information.

"Right. Austin, sometimes women have a hard time understanding what we are trying to do in life. They have it in their own heads what we are supposed to do and how to be, and try to fit you in this box you don't belong in."

I couldn't tell who or what Cliff was talking about, but I agreed with him anyway.

"You ever seen that movie, Scarface?"

"Sure, yeah," I said.

"When I first saw it, I must have been like sixteen. It was like, a message from God. Looking at Tony surrounded by all that money and power, it was what I wanted. That sort of fear and respect, and the money? Oh man, so I dropped what I was doing in school to build myself an empire, just like that."

"Sounds like a tall order," I said, not knowing what else to say.

"I tried to have a family; you know. Almost married a few times, none of them could see my vision, and no one wanted to stick around for it. They're the ones missing out! Me and Dale, got a thing going finally, come here and check this out," he said, pulling out his phone. "I know you're not a cop or nothing, so you gotta see this."

I walked across the stage, flicking ashes on the floor as Cliff held up his cracked iPhone. Blinking the smoke out of my eyes, I could see Cliff posing in front of the table of duct-taped bricks as he brandished an Uzi. "Pretty fucking cool, huh?"

"That's pretty sick," I said as he flipped through some more pictures of him with various guns.

"I know, right!? Could make over a hundred thousand a year if I wanted. I'm just trying to enjoy the process of empire-building, you know?"

Dale flicked his cigarette out into the rain and grunted loudly, pointing at his watch.

"Anyway, Austin," Cliff said, putting his phone away, "I hoped the smoke helped, but Dale and I got to get going. We got to see a man about a dog before heading out."

He held out his hand, and I shook it, not wanting to know the things these hands had done but smiling all the same. "Good luck."

"You too, brother, and look, if you ever want something harder than a cigarette, we are going to be at the Travelodge until tomorrow. Room 127, just knock twice and yell Austin, and I'll give you the family and friends discount on whatever you need. Still have to charge you though, can't build an empire on good faith alone. You know what I'm saying?"

I nodded and flicked my butt out into the cobblestone square. I didn't bother looking behind me as I headed towards the safety of the bus, and those two headed off on whatever adventure they were on.

Opening the bus door, I was met with bewildered looks from both Sade and Emily, who were sitting in the front of the bus. Everything had been packed up and strapped down, so I could tell they were waiting on me to get out of town.

"You...um...okay?" Emily asked from the passage seat.

"Yeah, I think so."

"Who the fuck were those guys? They didn't exactly look like friends of yours," Sade said.

"And since when do you smoke?" Emily followed up.

"Okay, well, honestly, you're never going to believe me. I had gotten into a fight with Sara and was blowing some steam when these two guys found me and offered me a prostitute."

Emily's jaw dropped. "WHAT?"

"I ended up settling for a smoke instead."

"Holy shit, that's wild," Sade said, shaking his head. "Probably best you didn't take the prostitute. Sex work is essential, but I wouldn't go through guys like that."

"So, the things with Sara didn't go well?" Emily frowned.

"I didn't even get the chance to talk to her about anything. She was just really pissed I was on the bus."

"The fuck, why?"

"Apparently, it is irresponsible of me with school and then Cameron and all that to be going out on the road. I didn't even tell her I planned on staying for the long haul or anything, just that I was thinking about it. She ended up hanging up on me."

A silence settled over the bus as both Sade and Em looked at one another, and as they did, it finally clicked for me too. Sara was right. For as much fun as we were having, how long could this last? If I really was going to leave on the bus with them, what would that look like for everyone else? For Casey in the apartment, Eric in the gym, for me at school only halfway through the summer semester? And Cameron? All of these things I never actually thought about.

"You know, love, the bus, we, Sade and I, we will always be here for you, no matter what you choose."

"I just...need time to think about it, okay?" I said, taking my beanbag chair out from behind the curtain.

"Of course, take all the time you need."

I gave her a halfhearted grumble and sank into my beanbag, my brain exhausted. I felt as though someone had kicked my brain from idle into top gear and I wasn't sure how to handle it. Even as Sade and Em made plans to stop at Steven King's house and then head back to Portland in the morning, I just nodded along, miles away. We were supposed to stay in Bangor much longer, but between the no sales and the forecast of more rain, it was only going end up burning money to be out this far north. So they came to the conclusion that it was better just to head back to Portland, maybe hang around for another day and begin the drive down south.

After halfheartedly listening to the discussion, I asked for the laptop to make to make a rather lack luster entry in my blog:

"Rain.

If I could describe tonight in one word that would be it. It's not that torrential downpour kind but, the more sinister type that lies somewhere between a drizzle and proper water works. The rain is keeping away the foot traffic and as we pack up with a whole $23 dollars in sales, it's time to head out of the city. Which brings me to another headache that is bus life...city...fucking...driving. There is nothing more stressful than navigating city streets in a 32ft bus and it takes teamwork and a lot of yelling to get it done. This is where communication is paramount because one mistake and your home and business is firmly embedded in the ass end of a Subaru."

Chapter Nineteen:
Long Way Home

July 29th, 2017. 2:03am

Jerking up into a state of panic in the pitch black of the bus, I thought I heard my phone going off. There was nothing as I blinded myself, trying to check for a miss call. With a sigh, I set my phone back on the floor and stared at the roof. There was no rain tonight. The only sound was the deafening sound of thoughts gathering in my brain. What was I doing here, adventure or escape? At this point, I wasn't sure there was even a difference. Taking a breath, I pressed myself into my beanbag. The night was cold for the summer, but summer was ending. It was almost August, and my birthday was just around the corner, and even then, I didn't know where I would be spending it. I could see myself equally spending it both on the bus and back in the apartment. The mental gymnastics were pushing my already exhausted brain back over the verge of sleep. The last conscious thought I had until the morning echoed in the dark behind my eyes. "Why am I here?"

***

"Good morning, sweetie," Emily said, walking past me on her way to the passenger seat. "Did you sleep well?"

"Yeah, it was alright."

"Do you want to go anywhere for breakfast before we head back?"

"Just some coffee and a breakfast sandwich would be good for me."

"Dunkin Donuts it is then! You hear that, babe?"

Sade grunted and smiled. "Yes, ma'am."

Pulling up my blanket back up around my neck, I watched the tops of Bangor's buildings begin to move as the bus rumbled to life and started the long journey. Even though Sade and Em tried to keep the mood light, the tension of not knowing if I was staying or going with them permeated every breath. They didn't ask me about it either as we ate shitty croissant sandwiches and drank burnt coffee. That was just as well because it wasn't until we were well on the road that I had an answer to give. Besides getting up to get breakfast, I hadn't left my beanbag. The thought from last night haunted me. "Why am I here?" If I could avoid answering that question, I would, but that was part of the problem. Avoidance. The gears were turning.

After Sara had left, something in the apartment had changed. Or maybe it was me. When her memory became a part of the architecture of our tiny studio, the line that kept her and one place and me in another vanished. If Sara had never stayed the night, if we never fucked on the bathroom floor, I didn't know if I would have ever gone on this little adventure. The rain had started to fall again, and the windshield wipers let out an obnoxious squeak that made my teeth involuntary grind in my mouth, causing me to almost lose my train of thought. I had spent most of my adult life running. Running from injury, from pain, from the responsibilities I left shattered around me like a broken mirror. I loved my time on the road, but how much of being out here was just those running instincts all over again? No. I was done running. I may not know what comes next. Sitting in my beanbag, I knew that being out here on the road wasn't the answer.

Eric's words from the base of the mountain came back to me, and I whispered them under my breath like a magic spell. A declaration. "Come on, the old life is over." I was going to stay in Portland. Stay in school and work on this life I created because I wanted to. I wasn't going to let fear push me away from this happiness. I needed to deal with my shit. I needed to deal with Sara and Cameron and this whole question of if we are still suitable for one another or what this family is going to look like if we get divorced. A surge of purpose spiked its way through my chest as my thoughts found themselves. It was time to stand my ground and act. The old life is over. There were still things that I was holding on to for too long. I could see myself with Sara in the future, just not like it was before. I needed her to know that. When we got back to Portland, I decided that I was going to call her and not stop until I got it all out. I wasn't going to ask for forgiveness or beg for her to come back, to let her know the man she married had died, and I am what remains. If she wanted a future together, I could see that not as we were, but as something new.

"Okay back there?" Emily asked.

"You know, what? Actually, I am," I said sitting up. "I just wanted to say that I love you two very much and I'm so grateful for you taking me out on the road like this, but I think I'm going to stay in Portland for a while longer."

"If that's what you want, sweetie."

My mind turned, still trying to process the words out loud. "I've just started rebuilding my life in Portland. I'm still in school, I got my friends in the gym and for the first time in a long time, I feel like I'm getting somewhere with myself. I want to stay with that for a while."

A smile creeped across Emily's face. "It makes me really proud to hear that."

"Sorry we brought it up in the first place. It just seemed like you could use the option," Sade said, looking at me through the mirror.

"I think I needed the option if I'm being honest. So much has happened and so much is continuing to happen that sometimes I don't even know which way is up. For the last few years, anytime things got confusing or difficult, I took the path of least resistance. This is the first time I don't feel like running away. For better or worse, I want to see where things go."

"Careful, you almost sound like an adult," Emily said.

"I don't know about that." I sighed. "But, for once I feel like I'm doing the right thing with talking to her. Towards the end of our marriage, we didn't even know how to talk with each other. It was like we were allergic to being honest with one another. I like not being afraid of it anymore."

"I'm so glad you came along with us," she said. "I hope that no matter what happens, that it's for the best. And for the right reasons."

I took those words, *for the right reasons,* and let them echo in my head. So much had been done out of fear up to this point in my life and if it wasn't for the hard winds of fate turning me around, I would have continued down that increasingly isolated path that fear brings you down. I used to believe that if no one could know me, no one could hurt me. What I didn't see was that if no one knew me, no one could help me. Love me. A person made of iron isn't a person at all. We are meant to be known. Meant to be loved, we are flesh and blood and bone, who yearn to be understood.

***

The gates were shut. Wrought iron bent into the shape of half moons and spiders shut the house off from the rest of the world. Two towering gargoyles perched on either side of the gate kept a vigilant watch as we approached the home of one of the most prolific writers in horror history.

"They really keep a tidy lawn, don't they?" Sade said, his hands on the iron bars.

"Oh yes, the landscaping is really beautiful. There are so many colors! And the house!? It's a Victorian DREAM!" Em said, swooning next him.

I sat back leaning against the bus and chimed in, "I'm sure they don't do the landscaping themselves."

"You never know," she said, without looking back. "Landscaping might be a relaxing hobby."

"If you were a multi-millionaire, would you do your own landscaping?"

"Well…maybe, depends?"

"Do you ever think they get weirded out by all the people that stand around and gawk at their house?" Looking

176

up and down the sidewalk, I could see at least three other couples taking pictures and shuddered at what it looked like on Halloween.

"I think after so many years, you just kind of get used to it, you know?" Sade said, turning around.

"No. I don't." I shook my head.

Sade shrugged, making his way back to the bus after snapping a few more pictures. "One more thing I wanted to ask you. Emily and I are going to get some ink done to commemorate our time in Portland, we were wondering if you'd like to get something done too?"

I hadn't had a tattoo since North Carolina but was really into the idea. My head immediately filled with thoughts on something to commemorate this journey I had been on since getting out of military. "Yeah, that sounds great. I'm down."

"We are trying to get matching ear tats. Something badass. What about you, you want to join the ear tattoo club?"

I shook my head. "The sound of that makes my head hurt. I have an idea though." It was only half a lie.

"More Viking stuff?" he said, pointing to the vegvísir on my elbow, which was supposedly an Old Norse symbol that acted like a magic compass. In that moment, I realized the sort of tattoo I wanted. Emily pulled away from the fence, taking once last picture.

"Can I borrow a pen and some paper when we get back on the bus? I got to sketch it out."

"ALL RIGHT, LET'S GO HOME!" Emily yelled throwing her fist in the air, walking past Sade and me back into the bus.

"Of course," he said looking at me through his round sunglasses.

***

Before sitting back in my beanbag, I grabbed the laptop from behind the counter and began writing out what I thought was going to be my last entry in the *Eventually Everything* series:

"No surprise: heading over to Stephen King's home was on the list before heading back to Portland. After being on the bus for a bit it made me feel bad for the guy, to be honest. To have all those people stop and take pictures and selfies with your front door can get to be a bit much. I understand it's not taboo to take a picture of the famous author's home, or the sweet bus because for those that stop by its new and exciting but from the inside looking out it never ceases to be a strange experience.

– Lone"

With that finished, I began a rough sketch of a bind rune that I wanted for my tattoo. This was going to be a celebration of everything I had worked so hard to achieve since coming home and everything I hoped for in the future. Interconnecting lines that symbolized rebirth, hope, fire, passion, and strength to be more than I was yesterday. To commit to this new life, I had made for myself. The rest of the world fell away as I drew and re-drew the lines until I found something that I felt connected with. The main feature was the arrow shaped Tiwaz rune, which pierced a network of lines that told my story. It reminded me of message in a bottle, except instead of hope being cast out, the hope was impaled on an arrow being shot straight at the sun. Satisfied, I let out a small yawn and fell asleep.

***

It was getting dark by the time the bus pulled up in front of LFK. I was half tempted to spend another night on the bus rather than half to walk all my shit down the street and back to the apartment. I texted Casey and let him know I was finally back. He was surprised I was home early, but I don't think he minded. I was still blurry eyed when he sent me another text letting me know he was outside the bus ready to help me carry my stuff back.

"I had a lot of fun, you guys," I said, shouldering my bag. "It really means a lot to me that you let me come out with you. I needed it."

"OF COURSE!" Em said, throwing her arms around me. "We loved having you. This isn't goodbye just yet. While you were sleeping, I did book us an appointment at Hallowed Grounds for the day after tomorrow."

"Wow, you're on it."

"She always is," Sade said from behind his glasses.

"Okay cool, yeah come by tonight or tomorrow if y'all need a shower or anything," I said.

They both gave me one last hug as I stepped out of the bus and back into the redbrick cityscape that felt like home.

Chapter Twenty:
Hellos and Goodbye

July 31st, 2017, 1:32pm

The tattoo shop was only a short walk from the apartment. I felt no need to rush as I worked on finishing the last of my summer school and staring out the window onto the street below. Much had changed for me in the three months since Casey and I settled into our studio. For the last four years, I had felt as if life was one long, dark night extended to infinity. A place to rot away until there was nothing left but, body left to wander until it too would give out. Since coming to Portland, going to school, meeting Eric, climbing the mountain, and being out on the road that inescapable dark was being pushed back with the colors of an oncoming dawn. That fragile hope had become more robust, like plant whose roots were stretching deeper into ground. I still wasn't sure if everything with Sara was going to turn out, or if I was going to finish school, but I knew one thing for sure. Already I was not the same person I was three months ago. That man died on the mountain top.

"Don't you have to go soon?"

"Hm?" I said, wheeling my chair around to face Casey.

"It's almost two, don't you have an appointment with your friends?"

"Oh shit, yeah," I said reaching onto my desk to grab the drawing that I had made on the bus and showed it to Casey, "What do you think?"

"I mean, it looks cool."

"That's it?"

"It looks *really* cool?"

"You're fucking hopeless sometimes," I said, putting my shoes one.

"It's just not my style!" he argued.

"What is your style hm? Some anime waifu with thick thighs?"

"I mean…"

"Alright, I'll see you later," I said shutting the door behind me.

Walking down the wooden steps into the shop, the place was an odd smell of incense and that eerie sterile smell of hospital hallways. From some unseen speaker rock music was quietly filling the air in between the buzzing of needles. Sade and Em were already waiting on me, standing over the counter talking to a skinny guy with a long hair and red bandana, his arm adorned in that Eddie Hardy style of tattoo.

"Hey!" Em said, turning to me, "Are you excited!?"

I nodded. "Oh God yes, it's been too long." It's true I was excited but looking across the counter at a pale faced guy getting his chest done, it dawned on me. Tattoos fucking hurt.

"Hey man, my name is Trevor," the red bandana man said, offering his hand.

Shaking it, I told him it was nice to meet him.

"Do you know what you want done?" he asked.

I took the small, folded paper from my pocket and unfolded it on the counter. "I wanted something like this done." He stared at my rune for a minute before shaking his head.

"You know, I'm probably not the guy you want doing this. I mean it's a simple enough tattoo, but I think it would come out better with another one of our guys."

My heart sank. "Are you saying I'm not going to be able to get tattooed today then?"

"Hold on," he said before yelling to the back, "Hey is Scry still here or did he go home!?" There was no answer and then after a minute a man came out of the back looking as if he had stepped out of a time machine from the sixties with his round glasses and matching brown suede hat and vest. As he got closer, I could see he was covered from his fingertips through his head with intricate lacing of occult and runic tattoos leaving only the area around his eyes and nose unmarked. There was an air to him that reminded me a lot of Eric, except given the look on his face I could tell he wasn't going to be as friendly.

"What is it?" he asked Trevor.

"Some last-minute work, if you're interested," he said, pointing at the paper.

"Interested being the key word," Scry said, ignoring all of us on the other side of the counter. I could see his eyes come alive as he looked at my drawing, he took a pen out of his pocket and started making marks. "Oh, oh yes. I'm interested. Who's getting it?" he said, looking up. I raised my hand.

"What do you think of it?" he said, turning the paper towards me. At first, I was pissed that he just drew over something that took me a lot of time and thought to make, but when I saw what he did, my heart stopped. It felt bolder. Deeper. The revamped drawing almost sang to me. I had never believed in coincidences before, but if I had been one of the skeptics, Scry being here would have been enough to change my mind.

"It's perfect," I said. The runes, the extra line work, he took my simple drawing and elevated it without compromising the meaning.

Trevor took a deep breath; he could tell I was stunned. "Yeah, that's what I meant. He's a like a wizard with that stuff."

Scry rolled his eyes almost annoyed at the compliment. "Anyway, we can start now if you want. I live for this kind of work."

"Let's do it."

It wasn't long before I was sitting in a chair across from Sade and Em who were getting the sides of their faces sketched out and Scry was free drawing the new rune over the top of my hand. That is when I knew something had changed. Another tectonic shift deep inside me which couldn't be undone. I almost didn't even notice when Scry's needle began pushing ink under my skin because for one solid second the world and its axis had aligned perfectly on the worn-out floor of that tattoo shop, and I knew that I was precisely where I belonged. Even as the pain came flowing back into my mind, it was laced with a sense of purpose, marking the journey so far, forever into being. A road map and a promise to never forget how I got to this point, but more importantly to find my way back if I ever slip back down into the dark.

After forty-five minutes, the three of us were crowding around the shop mirror, checking out the new art. My wrist was starting to swell, but that was okay. I still couldn't fathom getting the inside of my ear done like they had. Emily's line work was smooth and beautiful, which didn't look so bad compared to the bold black lines which dominated the left side of Sade's face now. Either way, it suited them perfectly, both together and apart the lines seemed to enhance what was already there. While I was busy fawning over the art with Em, Sade went back and paid for everything, including my own work.

"Think of it as parting gift," he said as we headed back out onto the street.

"This way you can never forget us," Emily said, giving me a hug.

"I wasn't going to do that anyway!" I said. "I really appreciate you both. You didn't have to do that for me. Seriously."

"We wanted to. Having you out with us was so much fun, but good things can't last forever and all that," Sade said, giving a rare smile.

"Listen, we got to do some things on the bus, but why don't you come visit after dark. We are for sure headed out in the morning, so it would be nice for one last night," Em said.

A part of me felt like crying, but I didn't. "For sure, yeah. I have to call Sara back anyway."

"Alright, sounds like a plan. Good luck with Sara. I hope you get it figured out one way or the other," Sade said, sliding in for a hug.

"Me too," I said. Still awkward about goodbyes, I gave them both a small hug and quickly began walking the opposite direction down the sidewalk even though my apartment was back the way they were headed. It was almost three in the afternoon; the summer sun was still high and not yet ready to fade. All around me, tourists shuffled their way along the brick, admiring the old buildings, and sipping their expensive local coffees. I felt as if I was existing in postcard or a scene of movie, which was giving me the energy to do something I had been dreading as much as I had been anxious about getting it over with.

Taking my phone from my pocket with my good hand, I dialed Sara's number, my feet picking up their pace down the sidewalk. My courage started to leave me three rings in and a part of me wanted to just hang up, but just as I began questioning myself, she picked up.

"Hello?"

"Hey. It's me," I said, slowing down.

"I know, what's up?" Her voice was shallow.

"I just had a new tattoo, so my hand kinda hurts."

"Oh? Are you back in Portland then?"

"Yeah, I decided to stay and finish school and all that. I mean, Sade and Emily were super awesome and I'm really thankful for them, but there is already so much going on here that I don't want to get up and leave it."

There was a short pause, "Did your grandma talk you out of it or something?"

"What? No, it was my idea?" I said, taking a left off of Congress Street and past the Children's Museum. My feet were taking me towards the ocean, I could feel it.

"I'm glad you were able to figure that out. I'm sure your son will be happy to know where to find you," she said, her voice flat. "Is that why you called me? To tell me you're staying?"

"Look," I said not wanting to beat around the bush anymore, "To answer the question you asked a while ago, yes, I can still get together. But, not like this. Not like it was before. If you really want to try this thing one more time before getting a divorce than I'm willing to try, but you can't treat me like I'm a bad guy anymore. I know you can't see it, and hell I can't always see it, but I haven't wanted to be that version of myself in a long time. I wanted to change. I am changing. Into who or what I don't know, but into someone better, and I need room to do that in a relationship."

There was an even longer pause on the phone this time, followed by what sounded like the shuffling of feet or papers, I couldn't be sure.

"Hello?"

"I'm here," Sara said, her voice strained.

"I don't know if you're going to be good with that or not. If not, I understand, Sara, I really do. I was such a shitty husband and father to you and Cameron that if you say that's a place you can't go, then I accept that and am ready to move on," I said, even more aware of the heat on my skin.

"I agree. Living in this limbo isn't good for any of us."

"So, what do you want to do, Sara? For what it's worth, when you were here last, I know it was strange at the end, but I really did feel something. It told me that we aren't dead. I still love you. I wish I could go back and change everything. Fix it up right. Not because it would spare me guilt, but because it spares you and Cameron pain that you didn't deserve. I'm sorry it took me so long to see that. It took me way too long to see past my own bullshit. But actions have consequences and if I've broken something that can't be repaired, I'm ready to deal with that, but you gotta tell me."

"You know, I always thought we would have this conversation in person. But I guess that's hard when you live five hundred miles away," she said. "I'll be honest with you, Cody, I hated you. For a long time, I found sleeping in the same bed as you nauseating and when we finally went our separate ways, I felt like I could finally breathe and that first night to myself after you had left, I slept like a rock."

"That's fair," I said, feeling the inside of my lungs deflate. She deserved to say how she truly felt, God knows she had put up with enough.

"But I think, after a few months of space, I realized that I didn't hate you. I hated what you had did to me. I hated that I have loved someone so entirely and they could treat me like I was nothing. That is what I hated," she said taking a breath. "But just like you, I'm not the same person I was either. I've changed. Part of that changing means tell you unfiltered how much you hurt not just me, but your son."

"I understand."

"No, you need to listen. If we are going to start again, I can forgive you, and I'm willing to put that behind us and try again, but before I do, you're going to listen to me. You're going to listen to all those things I'd stashed away because if I don't get them out now, I don't think I'll be able to start over clean because those words will still be in there."

The sun was behind me, I was making way up the hill to the Eastern Prom, the gentle green slope dotted with blankets and people enjoying the liminal space between land and sea, soaking in the warmth of the afternoon and the smell of salt. Taking a seat on one of the many benches, I took a deep breath. "Okay, I'm here. I'm listening."

For the next thirty minutes, I sat in silence while Sara let her pain out. Old urges cropped up to deflect the hurt. No one likes being the bad guy, but this wasn't about me. It wasn't about saying sorry. That's the instinct though, isn't it? To curl up inside ourselves, say we're sorry and hope that the pain just goes away after a while. To spare ourselves from having to reckon with the entirety of the hurt, we say sorry from a place of self-preservation. I had been doing that for so long, I didn't realize that it was denying her a chance to speak. Sitting under that blue sky, I sat with her pain the same way I had learned to sit with mine, holding it the way it demanded it be held. By the time Sara had emptied herself of all the words and feelings that had been snaking around the insides of her heart, the air had become cleaner. The space between us and the sky, from Maine to Pennsylvania had shifted and the great pressures that push in on us from unseen places had backed away. It was sharp change in that made it easier to fill your lungs.

When she was done, we both sat there in an extended quiet that felt a lot less lonely than either of us were accustomed. After a while, I knew it was my turn to speak, but I didn't know what kind of words need to be said after such a deluge of pain. Taking a deep breath, I just said the only thing that made sense to me in the moment, "What else have you been holding on to?"

"That's it," she said.

"I've given enough "sorrys" to last a lifetime. And I've meant every one of them. I guess now, all I can say is thank you for sharing with me. I know it's a lot, but these are places I never want to go again."

"Me either. Thank you for finally just listening. You've shattered my heart, Cody. I know there was a lot going on with the brain injury and all that, but those last few years were so much, for both of us."

"I know," I said, watching a sailboat off in the distance. "Even with all that. I mean now that you've said everything, do you still want to give this thing another go?"

"Yes. Before it's over, I want to know in the bottom of my heart that there was no way it could have worked. I would need that peace of mind, and right now I wouldn't have that," she said.

"Me either," I said. "You know there has been a lot of times since we've been separated where I wondered if you were thinking of me because I was thinking of you. Then I'd kick myself about it, wondering why in the hell I would even matter to you at this point."

"You've thought about me?" she asked, surprised.

"Just about every day in one way or another."

"I thought you'd moved on from me since moving to Portland. Thought that's why you never called or texted."

I sighed. "It wasn't that. Like I've said, I've said enough "sorrys" to last a lifetime. Every time I thought about picking up the phone, that's the only thing that would come to mind. This deep feeling of shame and guilt. I couldn't think of anything to say that wouldn't have wasted your time."

"None of it would have wasted my time," she said. "It sounds dumb, but when I came up, I thought it would be like it was in the movies. Where you'd see what you're missing and then turn around and confess everything to me. When that didn't happen, I thought that we were over for sure."

I couldn't help but let a small chuckle out. "It's not dumb. I'm glad you came up though because it made me deal with somethings about us I'd been avoiding for a long time. Maybe in that way it worked?"

"Well, what are we going to do now?" she said, the phone shifting in her hands. "Start dating like we're kids again? Five hundred miles away?"

"We've done distance before," I said.

"What about Cameron? What if it doesn't work out? I don't want to move to Portland and not have it work, you know?"

"What if you just come up twice a month to visit for now? Let's not talk about living places for a while, until we know, you know?"

"Yeah, that makes sense. Speaking of, I have to drive over to my mom's house soon to go pick Cameron up. They took him for the day since Jeff was home off the road, but I think we are going to all grab lunch together."

"Well, alright," I said. "How are we supposed to end phone calls now?"

"Oh, uh. Is it weird saying I love you?"

"A little," I said.

"How about we just say it this once and then wait for it to feel normal?"

"I can do that. I love you."

"I love you too."

After Sara hung up, I sat on the bench and stared out across the water. I wasn't sure how much could change in day, but it was a moment that made me realize just how liquid the world is. In one day, I got a tattoo, started dating Sara, and was saying goodbye to some really good friends. I felt though if I had questioned it for too long, I'd give myself an anxiety attack trying to comprehend just how impermeant what we thought was truth really was. I'd only lived in Portland for three months and yet, I was no longer the same person I was staring in the mirror back in May. If I could change this much in three months, I wondered who I could be in another three? Or who I would be next year? There was something terrifying about the possibilities. Just as I was sinking into the ideas my phone went off with a text from Casey.

You okay? I hadn't heard from you since you left for your tattoo stuff.

Yeah, I'm at the Eastern Prom. I had a talk with Sara, took a while.

Is everything good?

I felt a smile creep across my face.

We are going to try dating again. I'll tell you more when I get home.

Very Well.

Giving a stretch, I got up off the bench and shoved my phone back into my pocket. Before leaving, I couldn't help but look out to the rocks which I laid on not too long ago and the words came to once more, *Cody turned out alright in the end.* But this wasn't the end, was it? It was the beginning, the start of something new all over again.

Chapter Twenty-One: Promise

November 15th, 2017, 3:25pm

Fall in rural Pennsylvania was colder than I thought it would be. Perhaps it was because Maine was so much higher, I thought that the difference in temperature would be noticeable, but it wasn't. True to her word, Sara had been up twice each month, the last three months to visit. Roughly six thousand miles between all the there's and backs, but it had been worth it. Midterms were over and I had space to breathe in between schoolwork and this time I figured it had been my turn to travel. Dating each other again was a surreal experience. It was the same face I had known practically my whole life, but Sara was different than I ever remember her being. She was funny. I mean really funny and there was this energy about her that immediately brightened up the room. It felt like I was falling in love with someone new, and I'm sure she felt the same way. Laying in the same bed in her small apartment in the early morning light, it felt natural.

"So, what's this news you wanted to share?" Sara said, rolling over and looking at me.

"Do you remember that exchange program I was applying to?"

"The one to go to England?"

"Yeah! Well, I got an email last night from the program coordinator and she said my application was APPROVED!" I said sitting up.

"Holy crap that's awesome, babe!" she said, her brown hair catching the sunlight through the window.

"Thanks. I can't believe I'll have the chance to go abroad like that."

"Do you know how long you'll be gone for?"

"I think this one is six months," I said, frowning.

"But is it something you'd regret not doing?"

"Very much so. Plus, you get double the credits for going, so it would save me a semester worth of classes in the long run."

"I'm proud of you for getting in. You should do it."

"I'm going to. But it made me think of something. Well, something I was already thinking about, but this kind of would give it structure I guess."

"Is it about us?" she asked, I could feel it nerves in her voice.

"Yeah. I was thinking that, maybe, if things are still good when I get back from England, that we could move into together."

She sat up and looked around her room. "Like move into the studio with you and Casey?"

"No, I mean like what if we got our own place in the city. There are schools for Cameron and everything we need we can walk to. I don't know, I just think. I mean, I would like to do that."

For a while Sara sat on the edge of her bed, not saying much of anything and I could feel a tinge of worry, had I said too much? Was I moving too fast?

"Unless you don't want to!" I quickly added. "It was just a thought. If you're not ready then we can wait until you feel right about it."

Turning around, she smiled at me. "No, I'm just. I felt the same way, but I wouldn't ask you to move to PA."

My heart leapt. "So yeah? You want to move in together?"

"Of course, I want to move in with you!" she said, giving me hug. "I want us, I want our family."

"Me too," I said.

"Promise?" she said, sticking her pinky out. It was a moment that reminded me when were teenagers saying the same thing.

Taking her pinky in mine, I squeezed. "I promise."

"I leave for the UK in January, and I'll be back in June. I mean, the lease to the studio will be up around then. You might have to look for a place a little earlier, and Casey will probably have to stay with us while he's in school," I said, my brain rapidly going into a data dump mode.

"Whoa, okay slow down, hey we got time to think about all the particulars," she said, getting out of bed.

I felt myself get embarrassed. "Sorry, I just couldn't help it."

"I know," she said.

"Are you going to be okay leaving PA?" I said, getting up behind her. "I know your family is here."

"Yeah, but they'll always be here," she said. "Not to mention, there is only so much you can do in a town like this. I want Cameron to grow up meeting different kinds of people and having more experiences than what this place can give him."

"I mean in Portland we've got bookstores, museums, music, and history is literally around every corner."

"I know," she said. "That's what I'm saying is that I think it'll be better for him than PA. I mean, that's of course only if we are still doing good by the time you get back," she teased.

"I think we will. I mean, we've also done long distance before, remember?"

"Which time? As kids or as adults?"

"Both," I said, rolling my eyes.

"I know, I'm just messing with you. I think we're going to be fine too. Unless you find your true love has been some English girl this whole time."

"The queen's already married," I said.

"Guess you're stuck with me," she shrugged.

I smiled. "Yeah, I guess so."

Getting off the bed, I stretched and let my eyes drift out the half open window. Sucking in the cool air I held it in my lungs for a moment before letting it out slowly. For the first time in a long time the world was still and I allowed myself to sit in that moment of peace. It wasn't perfect and there were still so many questions to figure out, but for now I let it be enough. When you're picking up the pieces of an old life and trying to make them into something new, good enough can feel like a miracle. Because it leaves room for something new. Hope.

Epilogue

The thing about endings in memoir is that these stories don't really end where the page stops and find a place to close out feels like an impossible task. Because life keeps happening and its generally all messy. It has taken me four years to write this memoir and I am very much not the same person who I was when I started it. I think that's the message I want to end on. Change. It is human to change. Hell, every cell in our body is replaced by a brand-new one every six months or something like that. It might be a little more or little less, but the point is even our bodies don't sit still and neither should we. I spent years in this suspended animation of self-loathing and hate and that is time I'll never get back. Please. Don't be like me. Like I was. Don't waste precious time on hating yourself. We are not immutable. We are born to experience life, not to survive it long enough to die of old age or something else. If you were ever looking for a sign or permission to change, then here it is: The old life is over. It's time to move on and you deserve it to move on.

If I would have heard those words sooner, perhaps I could have spared myself and my family a lot of heartache. Learn from my mistakes. Learn from my pain, and when you get to where you're going, share your story and spare someone else the wandering in the dark. There is a lot of power in storytelling and in a world that seems almost over the top with its theatrics and drama, it's easy to discount our lives as not important enough to share and that's just not true. You matter. Your stories have value and maybe if we spent more time talking about hardships and lifting each other up the world would be just a bit brighter.